MW00478385

The Quadrille of Gender

The Quadrille of Gender
CASANOVA'S 'MEMOIRS'

François Roustang

Translated by
Anne C. Vila

Stanford University Press
Stanford, California

The Quadrille of Gender: Casanova's 'Memoirs' was originally
published in French in 1984 under the title *Le Bal masqué de
Giacomo Casanova*, © 1984 by Les Editions de Minuit.

Assistance for the translation was provided by
the French Ministry of Culture

Stanford University Press, Stanford, California
© 1988 by the Board of Trustees of the
Leland Stanford Junior University
Printed in the United States of America

CIP data appear at the end of the book

Contents

Prelude: On Reading Again

Reading occupies much of a professor of literature's time, yet this daily exercise remains deeply mysterious because of its extreme complexity. Following the example of many others, who have perhaps provided better answers, I too would like once again to ask myself the question: What is reading? As my title suggests, I would like to pose this question in a more precise form: What happens when we reread a text? For although I may read a text only once without ever returning to it, I have never been able to study a work without engaging in numerous rereadings. When I read a text only once, whether it fall within the province of philosophy, of literature, or of the essay, it remains inaccessible to me; I don't understand it. I don't understand what it wants to tell me; I don't understand how it is constructed. I don't understand how it differs from other writings of the same kind.

I had this experience yet again when I began reading Casanova. At first *The Story of My Life (Memoirs)* seemed to me merely a series of more or less curious anecdotes, apparently little related to one another. Since I had nevertheless been struck by the oddness of some of them, I began rereading these passages, once or a number of times. I remained puzzled until I was struck by the repetition of

---

An earlier version of this piece appeared in *MLN*, 101, no. 4 (Sept. 1986), tr. Thomas M. Kavanagh.

certain leitmotifs. Undoubtedly, if this repetition did not reveal the outlines of a structure, it at least reflected the steadfastness of a preoccupation. But only after additional readings did I become aware of the shifts between corresponding components as I passed from one episode to another. A nosebleed in one story, for example, became a defloration in another and an attack of apoplexy in yet a third. Or, again, in one story magic gave way to religious belief, while in another it took on the overtones of a blasphemous act. In order for these transformations and the principle behind them to become absolutely clear, I had to familiarize myself with the text in all its permutations. What I mean by this is that I had to be able to recall all its elements, whether my reading began at the beginning, in the middle, or at the end, because episodes like the ones mentioned above do not follow the same sequence within each story.

From these remarks I would deduce my first principle of rereading: *one must reread until the text can be broken down into its basic components.* This activity cannot be compared to the work involved in making a jigsaw puzzle. In the puzzle, the image is cut up according to laws that are not its own. I would imagine that when puzzles are manufactured industrially, the same cutting mold is used time and again regardless of the nature of the images, drawings, and landscapes offered to challenge the buyer's patience. The effect of rereading a text cannot be imagined in this way. If it could, it would be equivalent to photocopying a literary text and tearing the copy into pieces according to the impulses of a momentary irritation. We would then have reduced the text to its components. Reading, on the contrary, involves keeping the entire text in one's memory so that each and every one of its features can intercommunicate. This results in a feeling of haphazard multiplicity that cannot help discouraging us initially. But from this very discouragement the light will be born.

I would like to focus upon a decisive moment in reading, which often remains unnoticed and about which we very rarely speak: the moment when we feel we have been overcome by the immeasurable complexity of the text. It is piecemeal in our memory, and we are convinced we shall never be able to make anything of it, that it has overwhelmed us, and that our work as critics must come to a halt. During my study of Casanova (though I could say the same of many other readings), not once, after an extended rereading of one or many chapters, was I able to avoid the depressing feeling that I had better abandon my work, that those anecdotes were certainly meaningless and unconnected, that my previous hypotheses or my little discoveries were no longer confirmed, and that I had best abandon all hope of continuing. In fact, however, my passage through this moment of discouragement and impotence led to dawning light. Most often this happened at night or on awakening. In that mixture of confusion and extreme lucidity, an idea would surface, or a group of ideas would reorganize the whole of the text and enable me to see the structure I was looking for. If we so often have only a meager understanding of the texts we read, it is because we are afraid of encountering the difficult moment during which all our research seems to fade away. This moment of darkness, this passage through incomprehension, cannot be feigned. It must be real, and the text must truly have made us lose our footing and our feeling of mastery over it. There is no understanding that is not born of incomprehension—no understanding, that is, which is not somewhat creative.

The relationships that then appear involve, as do all relationships, links and breaks. Certain passages move closer to others in a completely unexpected way, while others separate from each other in spite of the fact that up until then they were juxtaposed. To arrive at this point, however, it is necessary to respect the whole of the text, to take into account all its components, even, if possible, down to its smallest details. I would therefore formulate my second principle of rereading as: *a text has been respected only when we have taken its totality into account.* This, it seems to me, is an imperative sometimes overlooked in criticism. It can happen that brilliant interpretations are given of a literary work, but the reader quickly realizes that the critic was satisfied with gathering from here and there in the text only those elements that justify a preestablished thesis or a worldview. Using this method, it is undoubtedly possible to pass in review the whole of literature and to demonstrate that it confirms the idea one started with—for truly great authors, at least, are sufficiently rich to have said something about almost everything.

Respecting the whole of a text is much closer to always expecting that we will discover we have been too hasty in the way we have connected or separated certain components. Most of all, it involves not being satisfied with our separations and connections so long as the whole of the text does not find a place in our interpretation or so long as even one element is neglected at the moment when we establish the overall structure of the work. This sometimes allows us to discover that certain details, whose meaning escapes us, are in reality of decisive importance I tried, for instance, to show this for the expression "dressed as a woman," which recurs repeatedly in one of the first chapters of Casanova's *Memoirs* (on which see Chapter 1, below).

In actual fact, we know that respecting the whole of a work is an unattainable ideal, but it can certainly serve as a regulating principle. An ideal is deadly and taunts us if we do not achieve it. A regulating principle, however, can guide us without being entirely achieved. To move toward the whole of the text, our reading should be endless, for we must move from the chapter to the paragraph, then from the paragraph to the sentence, and from the sentence to each of its parts. This is the way we ought to proceed. I did not very often take the time while reading Casanova to go into the analysis of sentences or into the analysis of a sequence of sentences. Whenever I did, however, I was reassured because I discovered that his stylistic devices are always in keeping with the workings of the text as a whole. Great writers reveal their particular style in all the details of their work. It is enough to make the effort to demonstrate this.

We now have at our disposal two apparently contradictory principles for reading: one aims to tear the text to pieces and the other to respect the text as a whole. Let us return now to the effects of the rereading or the continued reading of a text—one might say, of inhabiting it.

Have you ever happened to look at one object for a long time, a very long time, be it the leaf of a tree or a great painting? After a certain period the object in question disintegrates. It loses its global character and reveals pieces and structures that were not at all apparent when you first looked at it. If you were to stare even longer, you might end up asking whether you were not the victim of a hallucination. It is as though we ourselves, in a certain sense, become the support of this object, as though we were capable of recreating it.

I recall a book that made a great impression on me in my childhood. It told the story of a knight who had contemplated a mountain for so long a time that he became the mountain. A persistent rereading seems to me to be a similar experience. In a certain way, the reader becomes the text, he loses himself within it to the point of feeling, of being moved, of thinking and judging like the text, which imposes itself on him.

But, as I have just noted, one can also observe an opposite phenomenon, which occasionally takes place in scientific research. A biologist who, over a period of years, has observed a certain type of cell arrives at a point where he no longer knows whether what he sees is actually the object he is describing or whether his own brain and eye invent the object. The same thing happens when we have spent so much time with a text that we ask ourselves if we are still reading or if we are not reconstituting it in our own way.

Thus repeated readings of a text produce a double effect: either we lose ourselves in the text, or we lose the text in favor of our own prejudices and obsessions. The third principle of rereading can therefore be expressed as follows: *rereading involves a certain violence on the part of both text and reader.* If I read as a critic, it is so that the text will provide me with an explanation of itself, of its content, its structure, and its form. This is what understanding a text means, in the same way that one understands a leaf by examining it against the light and discovering how it functions, develops, and dies. In much the same way, one understands the human body today by submitting it to the investigations of modern medicine, which divide it into its component parts and photograph it from all angles and at all depths.

Yet why this violence? It is a response to the text's own violence as an artifact that presents itself to the reader to seduce and capture him, yet at the same time escapes from him in order to preserve the secret of its origin. I am thinking in particular of Diderot's great art in weaving a very subtle canvas in order to prevent the reader from escaping it and yet endlessly leading the reader astray in directions

Diderot starts but does not pursue. This becomes caricatural in *Jacques le fataliste,* but one could say the same of Diderot's other novels and—who knows—even of his work as an encyclopedist.

The author is duty bound to misguide the reader. Otherwise he could no longer write. Were the author to be aware of the reader during the writing, the reader's limited understanding of the text would trap the author and prevent him from inventing beyond the possibilities of this always limited readerly comprehension. The same is true of Casanova. The most impressive trick he plays on us is to have us believe he was not a writer but only a casual teller of tales. He also misleads his readers in making them believe that his subjects are purely erotic and that he repeats himself just as tediously as any other author of this kind of literature. I believe I have shown in *The Quadrille of Gender* the subtlety of construction and the extraordinary intellectual acuteness of Casanova's descriptions of the workings of human relations.

I do not wish to enter into a discussion of Casanova here, but only to emphasize that, like all great writers, he misleads his reader in order to blur the contours, both for himself and for the reader, of what he knows without wanting to know it. The critic, paid for knowing or for trying to know, inevitably commits himself to a struggle with the author as to a struggle with someone who tries not to give himself away, but who nevertheless provides all the means necessary for his being discovered, without which there would be no literary work at all.

If the literary text involves a strategy of revealing while concealing, rereading must also invent a strategy, adapted to the text and the author, that seeks to disarm the author in order to unmask him. I have already noted that one of the decisive moments in this struggle is characterized by the fading away of all mastery on the reader's part. It is at the moment when the author has succeeded in creating a doubt in the reader's mind about possibly comprehending the text at all that understanding has a chance of seeing the light of day. When the author has won, when the reader is totally disarmed, then the reader, who had entered the dark night of confusion, can return with all his strength—and then it is the author who has lost the battle.

Thus the link between author and reader, the passage from the first's creation to the second's understanding, takes place at exactly the moment when both find themselves disarmed and defenseless, lost and deprived of mastery. It is at what I would call this point of horror that they communicate with each other. I shall certainly not be teaching you anything new in saying that one of the characteristics of a great literary work—a work that crosses borders and centuries—is its capacity to make us feel some impenetrable aspect of human suffering, of the paroxysm and fascination of this suffering.

This leads me to the formulation of the fourth principle: *a reading that does not reach the point of horror cannot even suspect the text's source.* You will undoubtedly argue that this is hardly obvious in the work of Casanova. I believe I have clearly shown the opposite. Starting with the narration of his first childhood memories, we are already at this point: the shame of mistreatment, his terror in the face of a possessed and hysterical woman, the macabre games with cut-up cadavers, and so forth. If the reader pays attention, he will notice that the happy periods of love and power are followed by others during which the hero of the comedy descends into the most sordid depths of human experience. For Casanova days of splendor and vanity are never far from those of misery and failure.

It seems to me that we have understood nothing about Casanova if we pass over this point of horror. How otherwise, except from that point, can we explain the variety of the complicated strategies he develops in his relations with women, with gambling, and with magic? Everything is done simultaneously to avoid the return to the horror and maintain his relationship with it. According to his explicit intentions, he does everything necessary to escape from it, but secretly he arranges everything so that it will soon make its catastrophic reappearance. He would never have had the success he had, he would never have fascinated generations of readers, if he had been only an amiable comedian, an innocent swindler, or a cheerful womanizer. All his exploits were marked with the red-hot iron of the shameful, the sordid, and the repugnant. In reality it is at this point that the text reveals its unity. Nowhere else can we find the real connection between the three components of Casanova's existence: his hesitation about the differences between the sexes, his refusal to work, his fascination with superstitious practices.

If I insisted earlier on our encountering a moment of discouragement and confusion, it is because it is there that the reader rejoins the text at the exact point of horror where it tends to undo itself. But at the same time, thanks to this horror, the reader has arrived at the text's source. The act of reading must itself pass through the deadly suffering in which the author originally found the strength to create. Nothing is closer to artistic creation than the moment of anguish from which the work's production must originate. The reader must endure the same anguish if he is to arrive at the work's real principle.

(I cannot help referring here to the greatest American literary critic I know of, who has perfectly understood and demonstrated that creation is born of anguish. If you think of Harold Bloom's *Agon: Towards a Theory of Revisionism* [New York, 1982], you will be forced to acknowledge that the position I am now taking is patently obvious. In particular, his reading of Freud goes far beyond everything else written on the subject, precisely because it sees anguish as being at the very heart of the possibility of literary creation and especially of poetic creation.)

All of this can of course only serve as a point of departure for understanding a text's strategy. The author is transfixed at this point of horror yet never stops wanting to move outside it. One might even say that the whole of the author's work boils down to the double effort of moving away from this point while remaining as close to it as possible. The aim of every great work is to distance itself from this unspeakable suffering by speaking of it as precisely as possible. It is a construction that liberates from radical evil because it represents that evil in the universe of words, because it puts it before our eyes. The author takes leave of the unspeakable by speaking of it. He does not abandon it, because his work is its translation, its image, its representation. The work's failure to rid us of this suffering resides precisely in its letting the horror show through.

The whole of Casanova's autobiography could be read as an attempt to propose ever more complex montages so that he can hide from himself the abyss that constantly threatens to open under his feet. But of course each of these montages inexorably recreates the threat. One of man's points of horror, for example, lies in the loss of his individuality, which at the level of sexuality can be translated as a loss of differentiation between the two sexes. Thus, throughout Casanova's life there is no way of deciding whether his aim was to accentuate or to blur that difference.

Undoubtedly a hurried look, a rapid reading, leaves the impression that the libertine wants to exhibit his virility, but an attentive rereading suggests that this frenzy conceals a fundamental confusion: Is he not like the woman he is seducing? One cannot simply say that Casanova is afraid of women; what he is afraid of is not being able to maintain his difference and thus of being forced to return to a state of undifferentiation. But I think the situation is even more complex. Casanova not only has a fear, he also has a passion for indistinction, a passion for the horror from which he would nevertheless like to turn away. His first love relationships are marked by a complicated staging that allows him to remain unaware of the individuals and the sexes involved. And at the height of his love life he organizes a game for four in which all roles are interchanged. One sees clearly here how the writer wants us to believe there is differentiation through the multiplication of relationships he initiates; yet in making each of these relationships a form of the others, he wants to reproduce undifferentiation, to bring us back to the horror.

You will undoubtedly object that all of this has to do with Casanova's psychology and has nothing to do with the text, with its literary structure or with the work's strategy, which are all that we are interested in. I will undertake, however, to show you, both in the work's largest movements and in its smallest details, that horror and the concomitant necessity to state and to conceal it so as to better reveal it serve as the guide and principle of the text's construction. The style is both that of the person who portrays himself and that of the means by which he portrays himself. One could define Casanova's style as a synchronized game involving two hands, with one always knowing how to undo at any given moment what the other is accomplishing. In any single story, the doing and undoing are subtly intertwined without the reader becoming aware of it.

Let us look at one page where we clearly see this double strategy at work, an example I develop further in Chapter 12. Casanova is discussing here the prohibition of incest:

Along the way, the duke was the only one to speak, and he made a number of reflections on what is known as prejudice in moral philosophy. There is no philosopher who would dare say that the union of a father with his daughter is something inherently horrible, but the prejudice against this is so strong that one must have a completely depraved mind to trample it underfoot. This prejudice is the fruit of the respect for the law that is instilled in an honest mind by a good education; and, so defined, it is no longer a prejudice, it is a duty.

This duty can also be considered natural, in that nature inspires us to grant our loved ones the same benefits that we desire for ourselves. It seems that what best suits reciprocity in love is equality in everything—in age, in condition, in character—and at first sight one does not find this equality between father and daughter. The respect that she owes him who gave her life poses an obstacle to the kind of tenderness she must feel for a lover. Should the father attack his daughter by using the force of his paternal authority, he would be exercising a tyranny that nature must abhor. In orderly, natural love, reason also judges such a union monstrous. One would find nothing but confusion and insubordination in its results; hence such a union is abominable on all counts; but it is no longer abominable when the two individuals love each other and have no idea that reasons foreign to their mutual tenderness should prevent them from loving each other, so rather than making me cry, incest—the eternal subject of Greek tragedies—makes me laugh, and if I cry at *Phèdrè*, it is purely because of Racine's art. (F. A. Brockhaus, ed. [Librairie Plon, 1960], 7:231)

This page could be entitled: from horror to laughter, to better appreciate the horror. Let us look first at how it is constructed. Initially, the author puts in the mouth of his speaker what he himself or any other philosopher of the Enlightenment might think: declaring the union of a father with his daughter to be horrible is the result of prejudice. But since it is the Duke who says this, the reader can easily dismiss the opinion, which spontaneously goes against one's conscience. The horrible remains horrible, and one must have a depraved mind to think otherwise. Prejudice is a duty. Opening a new paragraph, Casanova seems to speak for himself, and he shows that the sexual union of a father and his daughter is an abomination. Then abruptly the argument turns on itself, the monstrosity is erased by love, and incest provokes only laughter.

In a sense, nothing allows us to foresee this ending, and, if one reads rapidly, as certain commentators have done, Casanova might, thanks to this text, pass as an ardent defender of the incest prohibition. But if one looks more closely, one finds Casanova's own particular style: what he does with one hand he undoes with the other. He weaves his text with two contradictory threads, which combine the horror of incest and a generalized laughter about the human condition.

Thus you see here the perfect coincidence of content and form. The fundamental ambiguity characterizing Casanova's thought is conveyed in these literary devices, in the way in which his story develops sentence by sentence.

With this in mind, I can generalize and formulate my final principle of rereading: *a text's construction appears most clearly when we have managed to pass from the point of horror to the point of laughter.* Laughter is the minimal distance from what is tragic in the human condition that the author has led us to take. We know this clearly from the great comedies: the real ones, those of Shakespeare and Molière, which border on the sordid and are just as capable of making us cry as laugh. Although tragedies do not make us laugh, they are certainly capable of exciting us and giving us pleasure through the very beauty they display and the catharsis they produce in us.

So long as our analysis has not led us to bring these two poles together, it is insufficient. We have not yet grasped the construction of the text we are reading. As I noted above, the question with which the critic is faced can be formulated as follows: How has the author managed to liberate himself from horror without abandoning it? In fact, there is no question of abandoning it. An unspeakable suffering clings to the author's body, and he must convey it in its particularity. A great text is one whose sole purpose is to convey this aspect of our destiny and yet to find something within each of its readers that will touch him because it is universal.

Reading thus becomes an experience of this horror held at a distance by laughter. What another has resolved we seek in turn to resolve through him. Reading is no longer a combat, but rather a complicity with the author; it becomes a catharsis, miming in reverse the process of creation. We readers are incapable of confronting the horror directly because we would not be capable of working it through to the point of laughter. It is better then to rely on somebody else who has given us a tolerable representation of it.

The Quadrille of Gender

Introduction

Octave Mannoni was the first to point out the link between Casanova and magic, * in his analysis of the strange episode in Casanova's *Memoirs* in which the impostor is himself taken in by the gullibility he had fostered. Upon returning to this text, I was struck by the structural similarity of various stories that at first glance would seem to have nothing in common.† I was sufficiently intrigued by these resemblances to want to pursue my investigation, and little by little I realized that, both in discrete units and as an ensemble, Casanova's *Memoirs* obeys carefully calculated rules of composition.

Initially, this work could undoubtedly be considered a pleasant collection of trivial anecdotes, sharing no connection beyond the temporal. A more assiduous reading, however, reveals the lines of force that truly organize the text. The author could not have been unaware of them, yet he took great pains to erase their traces because it was so important to him to present his writings as the fruit of the pure chance that had guided his life. He often plays, for example, upon the respective positions of the anecdotes, upon mi-

---

* "Je sais bien, mais quand même," in Octave Mannoni, *Clefs pour l'imaginaire; ou, l'autre scène* (Editions de Seuil, 1969), pp. 9–33. All works cited were published in Paris unless otherwise noted.

† François Roustang, "La Répétition d'un souvenir dans les *Mémoires* de Casanova," *Critique*, no. 285 (1971): 175–89. I shall discuss this episode at greater length in Chapter 7 ("By Magic").

nor recollections, and upon the brief introduction of short digressions, to create an overall impression that we accept without necessarily recognizing, and to produce glimmers of meaning whose origin remains obscure. Casanova fooled many people, himself first of all; his best trick was to keep the reader from taking him for a writer and to keep the French from considering him, an Italian, capable of mastering their language. These are the first, but most definitive, masks that he dons for the masquerade ball he is about to dance.

If the preceding remarks are justified, it will perhaps come as no surprise that, as it unfolds, this autobiography constructs, little by little, the figure of its author. It is as if the text were a projection of the successive movements with which one draws a face; accordingly, the *Memoirs* would be a film of all the gestures made by a painter doing a self-portrait. First we see a rough sketch, then nuances and complications, new shadings and perspectives. I hope to illustrate in several ways that, under the guise of nonchalance and happenstance, this work reveals a physiognomy of striking internal coherence. It then becomes impossible to distinguish between the development of the text and the development of the man. Thus there is no need to indulge in interpretation in order to decipher the two—we need only read.

Yet it is important to read the entire text, for there is not a single paragraph that would assume its full significance if isolated from the total structure of the *Memoirs*. Certain critics have painted Casanova in bold strokes.* They quote fragments and recount this or that event, but one never knows how they selected such passages or what one might extrapolate from their conclusions. It is for this reason that I wished, first of all, to follow Casanova page by page, chapter by chapter, trying not to overlook anything. One cannot pursue such an approach too long, however, without risking boredom—indeed, without the entire enterprise becoming monstrous, for the *Memoirs* contain more than 3,000 pages. I wanted to start by testing a method and then allow myself to treat more extensive groupings. The important point, initially, was to reconstruct how Casanova wrote. Once his style and approach had been character-

---

*See, for example, Robert Abirached, *Casanova ou la dissipation* (Grasset, 1961). Abirached writes in a lively style worthy of Casanova.

ized, I could use the results as a hypothesis in reading the rest. Often I have spared my readers detailed analyses of entire chapters and volumes. Such analyses would have contributed little to the readers' understanding of Casanova, and giving multiple examples would be pointless if I had not already persuaded readers that my claims were well founded.

The more time I devoted to the *Memoirs*, the more I perceived the work as a travel account that also constructs a character. By taking the ostensible form of a purely historical production, the *Memoirs* recall, for example, Schiller's project in *Ueber die aesthetische Erziehung des Menschen*, or Goethe's in *Wilhelm Meister*. Goethe had been greatly influenced by Moritz, whose *Anton Reiser, ein psychologischer Roman* (1785–90)—a very popular work in Germany—may not have escaped the notice of Casanova, who arrived in Dux in 1785. In any case, this literary genre was in vogue, so direct influence matters little. I only note these similarities in order to underscore the originality of the Venetian Casanova.

In fact, this *Story of My Life*—the title chosen by Casanova—seems to be founded upon underlying ambitions that are very different from the mere desire to set down on paper a succession of often extraordinary little stories. Casanova's work may well appear to be no more than that. But it also attempts what we might call subversion without revolution. Casanova suggests this as early as the Preface, where he presents himself as believing in liberty, immortality, and God the Creator—just like everyone else. Yet Casanova no sooner makes such affirmations than he empties them of all meaning, for he is anxious above all to laugh and to make his readers laugh. What he tries to construct is a free man—not in the classical sense, but rather in the sense of freedom from any obligations or constraints. He does not bother to upset the laws by which society fetters him; instead, he drains such laws of all force by subjecting them to ridicule. Through laughter and libertinage, he seeks to corrode from deep within, without disturbing the surface, whatever impedes his obsessive quest for total license: hence his need to wear myriad masks, so that he will never see his own transgressions. He also seeks liberty by willfully staging reality on the scene of his phantasms, where he can deprive it of all its imperatives, or by attempting to deny all differences, primarily the difference between the sexes that is so indispensable to the functioning of society and culture. Whether Casanova succeeded in his undertaking is another matter. His *Memoirs* are captivating precisely because they do not hide the vicissitudes of his project—including his failures, which always serve as an occasion to invent new strategies to preserve, more surreptitiously, the freedom to do anything.

The *Memoirs* remain a book full of stories—and they are true stories, whatever the author's aim. A great many specialists have verified the factualness of Casanova's assertions, page after page. The summary of such efforts given by J. Rives Childs proves that, even if errors or falsifications slipped in here and there, they are minimal in comparison to the mass of documents that were presumably involved in writing this immense work.* We shall see that certain modifications of history are quite understandable in the light of the intentions of literary composition. We know that Casanova began very early to take notes on everything that happened to him, that he kept all of the letters he received and copies of those he sent, that he often transcribed conversations the very day he had had them, and that he saved a mass of other documents concerning himself. Hence we could say that, to a certain extent, he partially wrote his story as he was living it, and that, while living it, he certainly intended to write it. When, in about 1790, as librarian of the chateau of Dux in Germany, he does begin to set his life story down in writing, it is, so to speak, already composed.

The twelve-volume manuscript was published in its entirety, save for a few lost chapters, in six volumes in 1960–62 by Brockhaus-Plon. Until then, the only known text was the one first published in 1826 under the supervision of Jean Laforgue, to whom Friedrich-Arnold Brockhaus had entrusted the manuscript with the request that Laforgue tone down expressions that might shock the public and correct language errors that would be inevitable for a Venetian writing in French. Laforgue was not satisfied, however, with merely cleaning up the manuscript; he tampered with the text from beginning to end. Two examples suffice

*J. Rives Childs, *Casanova: A Biography Based on New Documents* (London: Allen and Unwin, 1961).

4

to illustrate this, one an erotic description, the other a political observation.

Laforgue

After having prepared some punch, we amused ourselves by eating oysters in the most voluptuous manner imaginable for two adoring lovers: we placed them on our tongues and then took turns sucking them in from each other's mouth. Voluptuous reader, taste them and tell me if this is not indeed the nectar of the gods.   (Bibliothèque de la Pléiade ed., 1: 841)

Manuscript

After having prepared some punch, we amused ourselves by eating oysters, exchanging them when we already had them in our mouths. She would offer me her oyster on her tongue while I was feeding her mine; there can be no game more lascivious, more voluptuous, between two lovers. Indeed, it is comic, and the humor does not detract from the game, for laughter is created only for the lighthearted. Ah, what a sauce seasons the oyster that I suck in from the mouth of my beloved! It is her saliva. It is impossible that the force of our love should not increase when I crush it, when I swallow it.   (F. A. Brockhaus ed. [Librairie Plon, 1960], 4: 67)

Laforgue

In that day, Parisians imagined that they loved their king; they made all of the customary gestures in good faith and out of habit. Now that they are more enlightened, they will love only the sovereign who truly desires the happiness of the nation and who will be no more than the first citizen of a great people. In this it will be all of France, and not just Paris and its surroundings, that will compete to express its love and gratitude. Kings such as Louis XV have become impossible; but if such a king were to be found, no matter what interested party might promote him, public opinion would not hesitate to pronounce judgment upon him, and his conduct would be condemned before death had rendered him over to history. Kings and statesmen should never lose sight of this fact. (Pléiade, 2: 16)

Manuscript

In that day, the French imagined that they loved their king, and they made all of the customary gestures; by now we know them better. But deep down the French are still the same. This nation is made to be in a perpetual state of violence. Nothing is real here; everything is mere appearance. This is a vessel that asks only to go forward and that requires a breeze; whatever breeze is blowing is always good. Thus it is that a ship is emblazoned on the Parisian coat of arms. (Brockhaus–Plon, 5: 16)

Nothing more is needed to show that the editions of the *Memoirs* that reproduce the Laforgue text are outdated; such is the case of the Pléiade editions published in 1958, 1959, and 1960, that is, before the publication of the manuscript by Brockhaus–Plon. What is odd is that the Livre de poche edition of the *Memoirs*, whose publication was begun in 1967, should still reproduce the Laforgue text; it is all the more curious that the partial edition of the *Memoirs* prepared by Garnier–Flammarion in 1977 should again commit this error. Are there copyright problems, or do specialists merely want to continue reading the edition to which they are accustomed? This is indeed a mystery! Unfortunately, the Brockhaus–Plon edition has long been out of print. If, as I believe, Casanova is one of the greatest writers of French, and his language (notwithstanding its rare Italianisms) is beautiful, will not some editor give us the pleasure of being able to read the authentic text of his work?

I shall cite the Brockhaus–Plon edition, indicating the volume and page numbers in that order.

Setting Up the Love Scene

DOCTOR GOZZI also had a sister named Bettine, who was a pretty, vivacious girl of thirteen and a great reader of novels. Her father and mother scolded her constantly for lingering in front of the window, and the doctor criticized her penchant for reading. I felt attracted to this girl from the start, without knowing why. It was she who, little by little, kindled the first sparks of a passion that would later come to rule me" (1: 19). In April 1734, Casanova has been placed in a sordid boarding house in Padua; at the end of that year, his grandmother intervenes and sends him to live in the home of Dr. Gozzi, a priest and schoolteacher. Bettine, born in 1718, is in fact not thirteen, but seventeen, whereas Gozzi's young pupil is not yet ten. The romantic and thwarted love of a precocious adolescent, the first love that will leave a definitive, archetypal mark on all of Casanova's amorous dealings with women—this seems too good to be true. Yet does not everyone, when tracing out the first strokes of his destiny, single out one event that seems necessary?

Here is the story. After having spent two years studying with Gozzi, Casanova, along with his tutor, is summoned to Venice by his mother; she demands that her son discard his wig, and that Bettine be charged with caring for his hair. This is how Bettine enters the scene. She serves as hairdresser for the twelve-year-old child, and she washes him; but she also fondles him, which arouses and troubles him. He hopes for more and more of her favors. The magic spell is broken, however, by the arrival of Candiani, a new student described as a frightful boy of fifteen, "ignorant, vulgar, dim-witted, lacking any polite education" (1: 24)—in short, unworthy to be a rival. It is nonetheless he who enjoys the utmost favors of the beautiful Bettine.

Up to this point, the story is banal. And if it had only been a question of jealousy, this first experience would have been inconsequential. The incident is original, however, because through a series of farfetched events, Bettine will provide the young Casanova with a prefabricated image of a woman, of woman—of each and every woman. Caught between Candiani's blackmailing and the edicts of a bigoted and superstitious family, Bettine takes ill; she succumbs to "hysterical fits" (1: 29), to incoherent, comical, poetical babblings. Her family believes that she is possessed and calls in a long train of exorcists. They suspect that she has gone mad, and the physicians hold long deliberations over whether her madness could stem from a uterine indisposition. Calmed by a handsome exorcist, Bettine soon comes down with smallpox; she ends up disfigured, horrible, and stinking. Casanova, still in love, has by now mulled over his vengeance a hundred times and rejoices to see his beloved punished for her infidelity, so he inevitably assumes the role of the chivalrous servant. Yet as was also bound to happen, Bettine takes advantage of his chivalry and uses it to manipulate, subjugate, and exploit him. Although Casanova cannot stand to be the pawn of this woman, he cannot help being exactly that.

Despite the excellent schooling that preceded my adolescence, I continued to be the dupe of women until I reached the age of sixty. Twelve years ago in Vienna, if not for the timely intervention of my protector, I would have married an empty-headed young thing with whom I was infatuated. Today, I trust that I am safe from follies of this sort; but alas! that is precisely what annoys me. (1: 36)

Casanova recognizes, therefore, that he can remain actively virile by allowing himself to be seduced and deceived. This Bettine, whom he is "sure was neither crazy nor possessed" (1: 38), fascinates him to the utmost precisely because she had pretended to be crazy and possessed. He claims to be the sole person to hold this woman's (or any woman's) secret, and concludes that women are neither crazy nor possessed, and that they systematically deceive men; but a man cannot act upon this discovery—he can only use it as a guide, even as he is caught up in a vicious cycle of gullibility and deception. Women can only be approached as hysterics or witches; in that sense, their secret remains sealed. In order to deal with women, Casanova must not acknowledge what he believes he knows: he must deceive himself about the deception that he witnesses and take detours circuitous enough to let him avoid noticing the obvious. He will devise love scripts to ward off his phobia. These scripts, which consist in the endless repetition of an ever more complicated montage, permit Casanova to conjure away his fear of women by holding them constantly in view while seeing them only through blurred images that make both their identity and their gender uncertain—with the result that Casanova himself becomes uncertain of his own identity and gender.

Because it would be premature—and I would risk seeing my interpretation dismissed as a mere flight of fancy—I have hesitated to draw attention to a particular detail of this tale that might give away the end of the story. I can, however, no longer resist mentioning it, for this detail touches upon a plot that, had it only succeeded, would have avoided the drama and thus preempted the story. Sometime after the arrival of Candiani, Bettine stops coming to Casanova's bedside in the morning to comb his hair. He asks her, in a note, to explain herself:

Half an hour after receiving my letter, she told me herself that she would come to my bedside the next morning, but I waited in vain. I was outraged; but she surprised me at the noontime meal by asking me whether I would let her dress me up as a girl to accompany her five or six days later to a ball that was to be given by our neighbor Dr. Olivio. The whole table heartily approved of the idea, and I consented. I thought that this arrangement would afford a favorable opportunity for us to settle our misunderstanding and become intimate friends, without fear of any surprise arising from the proverbial weakness of the flesh. But then something happened that prevented our attending this ball and brought about a veritable tragicomedy. (1: 26)

In other words, if they had been able to attend the ball together, they could have made up, and Bettine would not have needed to fall ill. But a series of events unrelated to their story prevents them from getting there. The same invitation to the ball reappears between the two chapters devoted to this adventure (chaps. 2 and 3), accompanied by the threat that Bettine's illness will worsen should the plan fail. Bettine feels better after her first attack, and she plans to take part in a celebration to be given the next day. To spare Bettine, Casanova declines the invitation, but then receives this note: "Either come to the ball with me, dressed as a girl, or I'll show you a sight that will make you weep" (1: 33). And, in fact, a few days later she shows all the signs of madness. A third mention of this plan reappears in chapter 3, when they at last have the opportunity to make up. It is Bettine who speaks: "I suggested that you accompany me to the ball dressed as a girl; I was going to reveal the whole story to you and leave you the task of correcting it. This outing to the ball would have displeased Candiani, but I had made up my mind. You know what kind of hitch arose" (1: 45). One can easily understand how attending the ball together would have given them the time to resolve their misunderstanding. There would thus have been no drama, and no call for a "tragicomedy." And at the very outset of his love life, Casanova would not have witnessed the seminal spectacle of the woman he desires transformed into a madwoman, demoniacally possessed. If this had only happened, the destiny of this character would have been completely different.

If, however, we shift our perspective slightly and focus on the trivial detail—"dressed as a girl"—instead of on the aborted plan to attend the ball, we might come up with an interpretation that would shed new light upon the end of the story. If Casanova had dressed up as a girl, he would never have had to confront the figure of a hysterical woman or witch. If he had not been preoccupied with proving his own sexual identity, he would never have needed to be the dupe of women. This may be a minor point, but it is linked to something even more cunning: to a certain extent, Casanova learns his lesson and understands that, to avoid any future encounters with mad or possessed women, he will have to dress as a girl all the time, through a complicated game of identifications— as we shall see in the tale of his first sexual experience. At the same time, he will impose a long series of disguises upon women and, except in rare cases, will fall in love only with those who agree to make their own identity unrecognizable through various systems of substitution.

On October 1, 1739, Casanova's grandmother comes to fetch him in Padua in order to bring him to Venice, where he is to pursue his studies in law. At the age of seventeen—that is, in 1742—he is awarded the doctor of law degree. He does not recount any adventure with women during this period, except for the story of his vacation-time infatuation with Lucie, the daughter of the concierge in the house where he has taken a room. Lucie is ready to give herself to him but, although he spends several nights with her, he writes that he "respected her in what is essential" (1: 82). For Casanova to make love, he needs a ploy of a more complicated nature.

In Venice around 1742, as a young seventeen-year-old abbé headed for an ecclesiastic career, he falls in love with a girl named Angela who, despite her promises to marry him, leaves him pining away without granting the slightest kiss. Fortunately, Angela is the friend of two sisters, Nanette and Marton. It is these sisters who listen sympathetically to his complaints about his beloved Angela's excessive severity, and they who offer to act as mediators able to arrange a nocturnal tryst for him. The meeting does indeed take place, in the company of the two sisters. Casanova spends the entire night speaking in the dark, since the only candle had been quickly extinguished; yet however persuasive his arguments may be, he does not even win the right to touch Angela. By morning, he has firmly decided to turn his back on this woman, despairing of his ability to overcome her reticence. Several months pass, and, through a particular set of circumstances, Nanette manages to persuade Casanova to spend the night with the three girls once more. Angela never shows up; so Casanova takes advantage of the amiability of the two sisters and enjoys his first sexual relations with them. But let us not jump to hasty conclusions here without first setting the scene—a scene that proves to be rather complicated. For, in order to make love, this young man needs an extensive battery of props.

Casanova comes to this engagement neither to seduce the two sisters nor to let himself be seduced by them, but rather for the sole purpose of informing Angela about his disdain for her and of taking his revenge for her interminable stalling. He comes, therefore, in order to break with this captivating yet unattainable woman. He comes to exclude her and thereby regain his independence. *Exit* the seductress.

Moreover, he feels free to do whatever he pleases with the two sisters, for he is not in love with them. Indeed, after a few kisses exchanged out of purely "fraternal feelings"—which nonetheless excite them all—Casanova pauses to express these thoughts:

> These girls were noble, and quite respectable, and I did not want their reputations to be compromised by the stroke of luck that had placed them in my hands. I was not vain enough to believe they loved me, but I could safely assume our kisses had had the same effect on them as on me. Bearing this supposition in mind, I saw clear evidence that, with a little cunning and clever talking—more powerful than they could suspect—on my part, I could easily obtain certain favors over the course of the long night we were to spend together, favors that could have more decisive consequences. The very thought horrified me. I therefore imposed strict limitations on my conduct, and I did not doubt that it would require great strength of character to observe them. As I saw them come back into the room wearing clear signs of trust and contentment on their faces, I instantly adopted the same countenance, firmly determined not to expose myself any further to the fire of their kisses. (1: 97)

Despite the tempest arising in him, he is not and never will be a schemer who takes advantage of such a situation; rather, he wishes, as he will so often do in the future, to be great, generous, and above reproach. *Exit* the seducer.

Yet the seducer has hardly gone out the door when both of them—seductress and seducer—reappear on the scene in the most unexpected and uncontrollable form: thanks to Angela, the young abbé slips himself between Nanette and Marton. We find ourselves with the following schema:

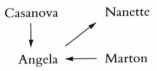

Casanova discusses Angela with the two sisters, asking them to explain why they are so convinced that their friend loves him: "Oh, I am quite sure," replies Marton. "In view of the fraternal friendship that we have pledged to each other, I can tell you that quite sincerely. When Angela sleeps with us, she calls me her dear abbé, all the while showering me with kisses" (1: 98). Casanova goes on:

"This naïveté so inflamed me that it took the greatest of efforts to maintain my composure." We can see what fascinates him: "Marton tells Nanette that, given my lively spirit, I could not possibly be ignorant of what goes on when two close girlfriends sleep together." As if the game of substitutions in the relations among these women were not already complete, he adds: "These remarks pleased me no end, and I told Marton that Angela should in turn serve as her husband" (1: 99). He wishes, therefore, that sexual roles could be purely and simply reversible. By rejecting Casanova's suggestion, Marton complicates the system, even as she reintroduces Casanova into the trio:

> At this point, she [Marton] laughingly tells me that she [Angela] was the husband of Nanette alone, and Nanette had to agree.
> "But," I say to her, "what does she call her husband during her moments of passion?"
> "No one knows anything about that."
> "So you love somebody," I say to Nanette.
> "It's true, but no one will ever know my secret."
> So I flattered myself by conjecturing that, secretly, Nanette could be Angela's rival.

This is the scene, or geometric configuration, that results from the conversation, in appearance the most casual exchange imaginable: Marton plays the role of the abbé for Angela, and Angela plays the same role for Nanette. All that remains for Casanova to do is to take the place of Angela between the two sisters, by accepting the roles that these women assign to him. He is to be the "wife" of Marton and the "husband" of Nanette; hence he, too, shall play both sex roles, by the good graces—and for the benefit—of the two sisters. At the same time, he identifies with the absent Angela, since he takes on the two positions that she herself had held in relation to Marton and Nanette. Because, on the one hand, he preserves his Platonic love, and, on the other hand, no longer knows if he is a man or woman, seducer or seductress—or perhaps because he is both at the same time—Casanova feels entitled to proceed to the act itself, liberated as he is of his own identity (since he is Angela) and of his own gender (since he is just as much female as male).

One last stratagem is necessary, however, for him to dispense with choosing between the role of "husband" or "wife" while making love with Nanette and Marton. After a prolonged series of comic maneuvers, all three of them go to bed "in the dark" and pretend to fall asleep. He has his way with them by pretending not to wake them, still not knowing which one is Marton and which is Nanette. They do not reveal their names until the operation has been accomplished. Casanova clearly does not want to know anything; but what underlies his refusal to determine their identities is a desire to avoid determining his own gender. He nevertheless refrains from developing a theory about this deliberate ignorance. All of this must be filtered through anecdotes or purely lighthearted conversations that attest to Casanova's passion for ignorance, undoubtedly stronger than his passion for women—that is, unless Casanova's passion for women is the most effective means for him to preserve and cultivate his passion for remaining oblivious of his own gender. We can foresee the further developments that the young man "dressed as a girl," first glimpsed in the adventure with Bettine, will have to undergo. It is (almost) as if this were the primary trait of Casanova's sexual technique. Perhaps all of this reflects something peculiar to his century and city.

In fact, the story of his success with the two sisters is followed immediately by the tale of a ball at which a certain Juliette, titular mistress of Count Sanvitali, asks Casanova to exchange clothes with her. Casanova would like to take advantage of the delicate passage from one outfit to another, but Juliette had not intended the exchange in such a light and ends up slapping him. This time, disguise is not enough, simply because, under these circumstances, doubt is not possible. If disguise had succeeded earlier—and is to succeed again later—it is because it contained an element of uncertainty; indeed, ambiguity is integral to the nature of a mask.

Another adventure arises that, for the moment, leads us away from the hypothesis I have advanced thus far and opens onto another, extreme aspect of Casanova's personality. When someone truly wishes not to know, he must convince himself that he actually seeks full knowledge and a clear view of everything. This new adventure contains a defiant challenge to incertitude. Casanova is invited to spend some time in Pasiano, a village in the countryside not far from Venice. His fellow guests there include a "newly married bride, nineteen or twenty years old," who rivets his attention.

He courts her, but she does not respond and flees from him. Be that as it may, here is "the curious incident that provided the drama's outcome" (1: 111). While returning from an afternoon drive, Casanova succeeds in finding himself alone with the pretty young newlywed in an open carriage. A storm hits, with lightning striking very near to them. "The horses begin to buck with fear, and my poor lady [who is afraid of thunder] is seized with spasmodic convulsions. She throws herself on me, holding me tightly in her arms. . . . I let her call me impious as much as she pleases, and grab her from behind by the buttocks, carrying off the most complete victory ever enjoyed by a skilled gladiator" (1: 112). It would be impossible to overlook this strange anecdote, which chronicles Casanova's second sexual experience, particularly since the conversation that follows underscores the link he seeks to establish between the course of the storm and their sexual intercourse: "She asks me how I could defy the lightning with such scandalous behavior; I answer that the lightning and I were in perfect agreement, and she almost seems to believe that this is so, and her fear nearly vanishes." And a bit later:

"Tell me that you love me," I tell her.
"No, for you are an atheist, and hell awaits you."
By then I had returned her to her place and saw that the weather was fine again; I assured her that the coachman had never turned around. I kissed her hands and made light of the adventure, telling her that I was sure I had cured her of her fear of thunder, but that she would surely never reveal the secret of my remedy. She answered that one thing at least was certain, that no other woman had ever been cured by the same prescription.
"Why," I said to her, "this must have happened a million times over the last thousand years." (1: 113–14)

Nothing more need be added to what he says here, except to note that he says it. First of all, in Casanova's eyes his gesture represents a clear challenge to the lightning, not to lightning as understood in this scientific day and age—duly interpreted, measured, secularized—but to the lightning that in earlier days served as a figure of celestial and infernal forces. The words "impious," "scandalous," and "atheist" do not appear in this passage purely by chance. Although they are pronounced by a woman, it is Casanova who gladly relates them. By ending the episode with the coachman's laughter, the young abbé would like to reduce its significance to that of a mundane story of buttocks. But he knows full well that he has played out this adventure on a grand scale and thereby braved a bit more than the reticence of a young newlywed; otherwise, he would not have referred to history, he would not have suggested that his defiant gesture is that of man(kind)—he would not have said that "this must have happened a million times over the last thousand years."

This woman is not the only person whom he seeks to cure "of the fear of thunder"; he also wants to cure himself. The superstitious magician that he will become (and that he already is) wanted to pull off a great stunt and proclaim this as his life motto: sex is the greatest remedy for the fear inflicted by the forces ruling our destiny, and man must defy woman in order to defy the sky and its storms. Far from reducing him to impotence, Casanova's challenge elevates him to the status of the lightning's equal. He knows that to conquer his fear of affirming his gender, he must make himself the master of heaven and hell—if only through derision.

In a more precise and limited manner, the answer he inflicts upon this woman is tailored to fit her exactly. To put it crudely, we could say that she asked for it, and that she got what she deserved by provoking him—albeit without knowing it—in an especially ticklish area. A bit earlier, she had tried to temper the abbé's persistence by giving him a lesson in morality, which only served to incite him more:

But toward the eleventh or twelfth day of my courtship, she plunged me into despair, for she told me that, being a priest, I ought to know that the slightest caress was a mortal sin in matters of love, that God saw all, and that she wanted neither to condemn her soul nor to expose herself to the shame of telling her confessor that she had sunk so low as to commit abominations with a priest. I replied that I was not a priest, but she defeated me in the end when she asked whether I agreed that what I wanted to do with her was sinful. I didn't have the courage to disagree, and saw that I would have to desist. (1: 111)

There is no doubt that Casanova was highly affected by such conversations, and thus sought favorable circumstances and an appropriate method for curing this young woman—not so much of her "fear of thunder" as of her bigoted piety—in order to spare himself from her annoying moralistic platitudes. For he persists in his torture so far as to make her admit the pleasure he had given her:

"Tell me that you forgive me and grant that you have shared all my pleasure."

"Yes, you can see that. I forgive you."

I then dried her off; and when I asked her to do me the same kindness, she complied with a smile on her lips.   (1: 113)

He demands kisses; he drags her down in his impiety. His greatest concern is to "secularize" this woman, so that she will no longer be associated with lightning; he would then have nothing more to fear in being a man.

In 1748, six years later, he attempts to raise the same question along different lines, in the course of an episode that we shall examine more closely in Chapter 7. Under the pretext of unearthing a treasure that has been hidden for centuries, Casanova undertakes a magical operation expressly intended to seduce the virginal Javotte, daughter of the peasant who possesses the treasure. Casanova does not demand that the decisive act come about through love, however; he asks only that Javotte be "obedient and submissive" (2: 300). He plays the high priest who is to deflower the virgin, not out of passion or need, but out of his singular desire to overcome the ultimate obstacle and thereby declare himself interpreter of the supreme powers. By a stroke of bad luck, a storm breaks out at the seminal point of his demonstration; he is petrified by fear, which in the space of one lightning bolt smashes his project to pieces.

Up to this point, the entire story is so utterly devoid of the most elementary common sense that one cannot help recognizing a typical trait of Casanova's personality, reflected clearly in this tale. He is attempting to reenact, six years later, what he had managed to pull off at the age of seventeen in his youthful sound and fury, when driven mad with rage and guilt by the moralizing speeches of the pretty newlywed—that is, identify himself with the forces of thunder, reduce a woman to impiety, and consequently proclaim his virility—but this time he tries to do it in utter cold blood, blocking all sentiment, exploiting the magic that was supposed to make him master of heaven and hell and, hence, of his own gender. Yet precisely because he is no longer acting in the heat of violent passion, this new unforeseen storm unnerves him so much that his eternal fear surfaces, and he is unable to take advantage of Javotte's complete submission. The sorcerer, and the male along with him, is in the end nothing more than a coward fleeing the taboo of virginity.

We now have before us two portraits of Casanova, portraits derived from the tales of his first two sexual experiences; they are beginning to come together after seeming at first to be diametrically opposed. There is more than a short passage, or obvious proximity, between the youngster who does everything possible to remain ignorant of his gender and the young man who affirms it by defying heaven and hell. The same fear is at work in these two portraits. This fear is visible in the second case because it is what allows him to prove his virility, even if it is necessarily the other person involved—the woman—who feels it. When Casanova seeks to confront his fear full force, as with Javotte, the results are disastrous. In the first case, the complicated scenario that we now recognize is intended to dispel any suspicion that Casanova may have a problem. We must, therefore, conclude that Casanova is not a Don Juan who disdains and mistreats women, thrusting both them and himself into a tragic register. He has confronted the tragic once before with Bettine, and he will face it again, but for the moment he has learned his lesson. Over the course of several decades, he will do everything in his power to suppress traces reminiscent of the possessed madwoman who could force him to live his life in a serious register. Thanks to his mother and father, Casanova is a child of the theater: he would like life to be nothing more than an inconsequential game. He will let himself be duped by life, enough for it to retain its spice, but not enough, or long enough, for the doubt that devours him to return and strike him in the face.

There will be other sisters, women taking on the appearance of men, nuns (sisters again), women to seduce by promising marriage, whom he will marry off to other men. Magic, along with gambling,* will serve to make both his fortune and his misery; similarly, his incessant traveling will serve to ward off the effects of time

---

*"Gambling is merely the realm of belief and mystification in which Casanova evolved, for he was not truly a gambler, and his taste for mystification leads one to assume that he would not have minded being mystified." René Tostain, "Le Joueur, essai psychanalytique," *L'Inconscient*, no. 2 (April 1967): 125.

on his body, for he must always fend off the tragic. Like everyone (but in a more caricatural way than most), Casanova is dedicated to repetition. He complicates his scenarios, but always seeks to act out the same one. Time nonetheless catches up with this traveler turning in circles; and at the beginning of his *Memoirs*, after having recounted his first recollections, he makes the following fundamental assertion: there is a force in our imagination endlessly striving to express itself through schemata and processes that escape our understanding. And he underscores this point by writing: "Many things become real that only existed beforehand in our imagination, and consequently many effects that might have been attributed to faith may not always be miraculous. They are miracles, however, for those who lend to faith a boundless power" (1: 6).

The Perfect Alibi

THE STORY of Casanova's first loves takes up chapters 2–5 of the *Memoirs*. If women no longer play the same central role in chapters 6 and 7, which recount the young abbé's quarrels with his tutors, the art of evasion is nonetheless displayed there just as forcefully.

Early in 1743, after having spent some time in the countryside, Casanova returns to Venice. His life takes a decisive turn as a result of two events. In March, his maternal grandmother—who had taken care of him since his childhood, protected him, and spent all that she had for him—dies. From that point on, barely eighteen years old, he is left to his own resources, without a hearth or home, deprived of any relative or friend to restrain him within proper bounds or offer him a possible refuge. The situation is aggravated by the second important event in Casanova's life: in April, his mother, an actress who is constantly traveling, decides to give up the house that she had maintained in Venice and sell all the furniture (1: 115). It is this decision that provokes, or at least accentuates, a singular behavior pattern in Casanova, which will soon lead him into a series of disputes with authority figures. Through his account of these confrontations, he reveals a side of himself that we have not yet encountered, a particular way of understanding legality and of contending with other men. Here is an example of his very personal way of presenting the facts:

When I learned that at the end of the year I would be homeless, and that all of the furniture would be sold, I took no more pains to be frugal. I had already sold some linen, tapestries, and porcelain; the task at hand now was to dispose of the mirrors, the beds. I knew that my conduct would be viewed with disapproval, but also knew that all of these things were inherited from my father, and that my mother had no rightful claim to them. I thus considered myself to be the master. As for my brothers, there would be plenty of time for us to discuss the matter. (1: 116)

This casualness is all the more remarkable when compared with the wording of the preceding passage:

She [his mother] told me [in a letter] that she had communicated her intentions to Abbé Grimani, and that I was to follow his wishes in everything. He was instructed to sell all of the furniture and to place me, as well as my brothers and sister, in a good boarding school. I called upon Grimani at his home to assure him that I would always respect his orders. The rent of the house had been paid until the end of the year. (1: 115–16)

Hence Casanova initially presents himself as a son who always obeys his mother and the man she has appointed to carry out her instructions. But it becomes clear a moment later that he intends to follow nothing but his own whims, justified with specious excuses. First of all, he sells whatever he pleases without waiting to be informed that the house is to be closed. Furthermore, in doing so, he knows that he is slighting his brothers. But on the other hand, he also knows that he can use his gifts as a fast-talker to soothe and placate them. From the abandoned boy lacking hearth and home, Casanova swiftly becomes a young man without faith or law.

The operation is obviously not innocent. He not only scorns his mother's specific wishes and disregards his brothers' rights, but also dissipates his father's inheritance before he has even received it, judging himself to be its sole master. Others might have honored the memory of their parents by finding a safe place in which to keep some of the family possessions. Casanova never lets up in his efforts to erase the traces of his origins, just as he will later abandon at each turn all witnesses to his past. He will retain only his papers, the letters he had received, copies of those he had sent, and fragments of stories. For one of the great passions that possess him is to be free of any mother or father, free of any genealogy other than the one concocted for his theater, free of the marks of any history save that inscribed in a script. The seducer must be free of all attachments if he is to succeed in making all kinds of promises without committing himself to any—so that he can live out his scenarios, one after the other.

As Casanova had predicted, M. Grimani does not take kindly to his pillage. He sends a man named Razzetta to sell the furniture, and when Casanova protests, he has it placed under seal. This brings on the fury of the young abbé, who goes out to find himself a lawyer. But Grimani stands firm and breaks the resistance of his young charge. After another adventure, the very same Grimani arranges for Casanova to be confined in Fort Saint-André and has the order carried out by none other than Razzetta. Several weeks later, Casanova takes his revenge. One night, after having set up a perfect alibi, Casanova sneaks into Venice, finds Razzetta alone in the street, beats him black-and-blue, and returns to the fort incognito. It is a real pleasure to read and reread this tragicomic exploit, which so aptly reveals the methods of our hero. He accomplishes his revenge so well that everyone is quite aware who might have broken Razzetta's nose and some of his teeth, yet all are obliged to accept the evidence that Casanova had nothing to do with it.

Casanova's cunning is double. He takes his revenge on Razzetta, but without being discovered; and he makes it known that he is avenged, but in a way that no one can accuse him of it. Moreover, by attacking Razzetta, who is merely acting on orders, he saves himself the trouble of directly taking on the authority who lies behind everything, namely M. Grimani. When he finds himself face to face with Grimani, Casanova always behaves obediently and promises to accept the conditions proposed to him; but he does as he pleases behind Grimani's back. His goal, which he successfully accomplishes, is to make people laugh at authority, to ridicule it, without ever confronting it directly.

This is a constant leitmotiv in these chapters. When he is thrown out of his living quarters by M. Malipiero, his protector of the moment, for having taken too many liberties with a young girl living there, Casanova sends this note to defend himself: "You struck me out of anger, and for this reason you cannot boast of having taught me a lesson. So I have not learned anything. To forgive you, I would have to forget that you are a man of wisdom; and

I shall never forget that" (1: 119). To which he adds this comment, for the benefit of the reader: "This gentleman may have been right; but with all of his prudence he handled the affair badly, for all of his domestics guessed why he had exiled me, and he became the laughingstock of the whole city."

His attitude toward authority is irreproachable. He recognizes Malipiero's wisdom and would never question it, since he will never forget it. The approach he has taken nonetheless has two results that are equally valuable in Casanova's eyes: he has learned nothing, and everyone has had a good laugh.

The fact that he has learned nothing is essential, not only because he thereby owes nothing—or at least is in no way indebted to his benefactor—but also because it enables him to remain a novice, with no experience or memory, ever entitled to repeat himself and start over from scratch. The expression "I have not learned anything" could well be one of the most fitting descriptions of this character—an eternal adolescent who will never grow up, a greenhorn actor who will find himself decades later on the same stage in the same role. The same expression—proof that Casanova is fond of saying it—had already been used on the preceding page at the end of the advice given by Malipiero: "Although I was following the maxims of this school [the Stoic philosophers that Malipiero had praised], an incident occurred a month afterward that cost me his friendship, and that taught me nothing" (1: 118).

The fact that Malipiero "became the laughingstock of the whole city" is just as amusing for Casanova. For, even while he must respect authority and venerate its wisdom, this "badly handled" authority must degrade itself without implicating Casanova in the least. First, he protects himself from any guilt that could be incurred by rebelling against a figure of power. Second, he draws our attention to the fact that this authority figure has reduced himself to impotence by inviting ridicule; Casanova remarks that he need not subscribe to its lesson.

Casanova nevertheless comments that Malipiero "gave me a lesson that I have never forgotten" (1: 117). Yet far from contradicting the above analysis, this lesson confirms it, for, by following Malipiero's words to the letter, Casanova is able to live in a perfect state of alibi under all circumstances—at a moment's notice, he can be conveniently distant from the scene of the "crime" and absolve himself of any blame for what occurs. Here is the lesson:

> "The famous precept of the Stoic philosophers," he said to me, "can be perfectly explained by these words: 'Give yourself up to whatever fate offers you, provided you do not feel an invincible repugnance to accepting it.'"
>
> He added that this was the genius of Socrates, *Saepe revocans raro impellens*, and that it was the origin of the *fata viam inveniunt* of the Stoics. (1: 117)

To resign himself to fate, trust in destiny as his sole guide, and submit to Fortune—such expressions, which recur frequently throughout the *Memoirs*, express Casanova's unparalleled knack for avoiding any responsibility, for situating himself indefinitely on the margins, for having (once again) nothing to do with the matter at hand, for blithely accepting his fate without resistance, and for doing nothing except when obliged. Casanova is, still and always, like an actor on stage who is not the author of his actions, but simply someone playing a role that he did not invent, a role dictated purely by the rhythm of his improvisations. Thanks to destiny and chance, Casanova is accountable for nothing and need not worry about history, even less about its significance; for the weight of experience is minimal, since it appears only in the text of a tale. Casanova's masterstroke is to have been an actor not on the stage, like his father and mother, but in real life.

We find him having recourse once again to laughter and derision in the story of his brief stay in a seminary. His mother writes to him (1: 116) to say that she has obtained the nomination of a monk to the bishopric of Calabria; the new bishop has pledged in return to take the young Casanova under his wing and help him along in his ecclesiastic career. While waiting for the bishop, the young abbé takes temporary lodging in the home of a dancer; but because this situation is not appropriate for a young man of his condition, he is taken to a seminary. Upon entering the seminary, Casanova must undergo an examination to determine his level; but because he is a *Doctor in utroque* (a doctor in both civil and canon law)—and does not deign to make this known—he plays the idiot out of spite and ends up being placed among the children of the grammar class. A fortuitous meeting with one of his old instructors unveils the comedy that he had played:

"Why did you feign such ignorance at the examination?" the rector asked me.

"Why were you so unjust as to compel me to take it?"

He looked annoyed and escorted me to the dogmatics school, where my dormitory mates received me with great astonishment. After dinner, during recess, they befriended me, gathered around me, and put me in a fine mood.   (1: 126)

The rector is the first to be subjected to Casanova's ridicule. Next comes the inevitable dormitory episode. One night, Casanova gets up to go to the "cloakroom" (1: 129), and as he is returning, he stops to visit a friend. As luck would have it, the watchman awakens from his snoring and sets out to make a round; Casanova hurries back to his bed, only to find it occupied by a neighbor who had gotten up for the same reason, lost his way back in the dark, and slipped into Casanova's empty bed by mistake. The watchman finds both of them in the same bed. The next day, the two seminarians are interrogated, judged guilty, and whipped:

The moment my hands were free, I asked the rector whether I could write two lines at the foot of the crucifix. He gave orders to bring ink and paper, and this is what I wrote:

"I swear by this God that I have never spoken to the seminarian who was found in my bed. As an innocent person, I must therefore protest and appeal to the father superior to correct this shameful violence."

My comrade in misery signed my letter of protest, and I asked the pupils gathered there whether anyone could refute what I had sworn in writing. With one voice, they immediately declared that we had never been seen conversing together, and that no one knew who had put the lamp out. The rector left the room, speechless, in the midst of hisses and boos; but he sent us to prison all the same on the fifth floor of the convent, in separate quarters. An hour later they brought up my bed and all my belongings, and my meals were brought to me every day. On the fourth day, the curate Tosello came for me with instructions to take me to Venice. I asked if he had looked into my case; he told me that he had just spoken to the other seminarian, knew all the details, and believed we were both innocent; but he did not know what could be done about it. "The rector," he told me, "does not like to be wrong."   (1: 131–32)

Casanova truly stages the incident skillfully. He not only enjoys himself and gives his companions a good laugh, but also succeeds in turning the situation around: he inspires a small revolt from the

non-incriminating position of the wrongfully accused and undermines respect for authority in his own eyes as well as in the eyes of
everyone else. Above all, he succeeds in dismissing one authority
after another: the curate Tosello, who had a hand in putting Casanova in the seminary, recognizes the innocence of his protégé; and
as for the rector, he sinks deeper and deeper in his wrongdoing.

It is no surprise that these chapters, which are primarily concerned
with settling accounts and belittling authority, unfold against the
background of a sexual tonality very different from that of the preceding chapters. Nothing goes well with women anymore. When
he is caught with Thérèse Imer trying to "examine the differences
of configuration between a girl and a boy" (1: 119), Casanova is
thrown out of the home of his benefactor, Malipiero; when he is
with his angels Nanette and Marton, he is either impotent (1:
132–33) or in such a state that he cannot pay them homage (1: 141),
for a beautiful Greek slave woman has left him with an unpleasant
souvenir that lingers six weeks (1: 135–40); he is led on by Mme
Vida, the sister of the major at Fort Saint-André (1: 140); and to top
it all off, the daughter of the count of Bonafede, a desirable young
beauty whom he meets at the fort, is transformed into an ugly slat-
tern who horrifies him (1: 148–57). He dwells so long upon this
last episode—ending it with some melancholy reflections on the
effects of appearance ("I compared reality with the imagination and
had to give the preference to the latter, for reality is always depen-
dent on it")—that one is left with the conclusion that his system of
seduction can no longer function under the weight of his comprehensive criticism of authority; for reality monopolizes his energies
in his fight against the powers that be.

His vexations with women serve here as the necessary corollary
to his youthful homosexuality. It is no mere coincidence that the
description of his brief stay in the seminary—barely fifteen days—
dominates these chapters, or that the longest development concerns
the obsession with dormitory life that is characteristic of the school-
masters and students alike. Casanova's only happy attachment during these months is the following:

A handsome seminarian, about fifteen years old, who must be a bishop
today (if he is not already dead), captured my attention as much for his fine
features as for his talent. He aroused the strongest feelings of friendship in

me, and during recess, instead of playing skittles with the others, we would stroll alone together. We conversed about poetry. . . . In four days we became such fast friends that we were jealous of each other and would sulk whenever one of us left the company of the other in order to take a walk with someone else.   (1: 126–27)

It is this friend who comes to visit him one evening, a visit that Casanova returns a few nights later, bringing on the rector's wrath and resulting in Casanova's expulsion from the seminary. The handsome seminarian acts as a sort of anti-Razzetta in this chapter, as the figure of the well-loved man with whom Casanova converses, laughs, and enjoys himself—in opposition to the man who represents tyranny (1: 125, 132). It is significant that the episode of the seminarian is situated here as an interlude in the dispute with Razzetta, between the moment when Razzetta has seals put on the doors of the house and the scene in which he sends Casanova off to Fort Saint-André, where Casanova will plan his revenge.

We should not underestimate the art and precision involved in Casanova's account of his adventures in the seminary. Casanova is a great storyteller who leaves nothing to chance. When he does stray from his subject, it is undoubtedly to charge the plot with extra anecdotes; although such anecdotes may seem unrelated, they serve to articulate another aspect of his character and another clue to his vision of existence. The seminary is a voluntary prison that foreshadows another prison, this one involuntary: the fort. But for Casanova, the same tyranny is at work, the tyranny of powerful figures who abuse their authority (he will later draw attention to the fact that the inheritance he was supposed to receive from Grimani after the sale of the furniture proves to be a hoax; 1: 141). Casanova's love for the handsome seminarian and the shouts of the other pupils heckling the rector are a counterpoint to Casanova's hatred for Razzetta. Casanova's constant misadventures with women indicate that, in his revolt against authority, he is completely wrapped up in rivalry with other men. Casanova surely does not wish to prove anything, as would a moralist writer; so we can read him without suspecting his intentions. He nonetheless employs very crafty writing techniques to draw his unwitting reader into the huge enterprise that he has undertaken; his project is an indirect, cleverly disguised denial of the foundations of society, a refusal to take part in the grotesque history of humanity—a refusal that entails accepting any risks he might incur. One particular risk is to find that his success with women is hindered by concentrating all of his energies upon ridiculing authority figures, for acting on the side of reality saps the imagination necessary for seduction. One risks sinking into the sordid as a consequence, which is precisely what will soon happen to Casanova.

Although the tone of these chapters is different from that of the preceding chapters, we find the same art of evasion. Just as Casanova apparently wanted to know nothing of the differences between genders or between individuals in his earlier dealings with women, so too does he act as a rival of authority and its representatives here, all the while carefully donning the mask of innocence. At the seminary, he is judged guilty when he is innocent; in the Razzetta affair, he is guilty but arranges things so as to appear innocent. It is of the utmost importance for him to blur the distinction between guilt and innocence, to avoid being accused of being too serious and reproached for seeking to construct a counterhistory. He would then be no more than a tragic rebel figure. It is precisely the tragic that he wants to eliminate from his existence. So he settles for turning all of this into a narrative, to laugh about it and make his readers laugh—as he puts it, to attract good company (1: 135–36).

All of this seems inseparable from one of the two childhood recollections that he relates at the beginning of his *Memoirs*. This passage should be quoted in its entirety because it illustrates so well the way in which Casanova uses rivalry, and because it conforms so closely to the episodes I have just discussed:

> The second circumstance of any importance that I remember happened three months after my trip to Murano, six weeks before my father's death. I give it to my reader to convey some idea of the manner in which my character was expanding.
>
> One day toward the middle of November, I was with my brother François, two years younger than I, in my father's room, watching him attentively as he was working at optics. A large lump of crystal, round and cut into many facets, was lying on the table and caught my attention. I was enchanted to find that, if I held it near my eyes, it multiplied objects. I noticed that no one was watching me and seized the occasion to put it in my pocket.

Three or four minutes after this, my father got up to fetch the crystal; when he did not find it, he naturally accused one of us of having taken it. My brother assured him that he had not touched it, and although I was guilty, I did the same; whereupon my father said that we should be searched, and threatened the liar with a good thrashing. After pretending to hunt for the crystal in every corner of the room, I slyly slipped it into my brother's pocket. At first I was sorry for what I had done, for I might just as easily have pretended to have found the crystal somewhere about the room; but the deed was done. My father grew impatient with our futile efforts, searched us, found the crystal on the innocent boy, and administered the promised thrashing. Three or four years later, I was foolish enough to boast before my brother of the trick that I had played on him. He never forgave me and never missed an opportunity to take his revenge.

While giving my confession sometime later, I told the priest about this crime in great detail and gained some knowledge that afforded me great satisfaction. My confessor, who was a Jesuit, told me that by that deed I had verified the meaning of my first name, Jacques, which in Hebrew means "supplanter." It is for that reason that God had changed the name of the ancient patriarch Jacob to Israel, which means "seer." He had deceived his brother Esau.

Six weeks after this adventure, my father was stricken by an abcess in his head near one ear, which carried him off in eight days.   (1: 6–7)

The fact that Casanova limits himself to relating two childhood memories in the first chapter of his *Memoirs* signals that they should be examined closely, particularly given that, in announcing the second incident (just cited), Casanova adds that he has chosen it "to convey some idea of the manner in which my character was expanding." In other words, this is a typical recollection, representative of his persona.

Curiously, Casanova places the tale of the stolen crystal between two references to his father's death. We read at the beginning: "Six weeks before my father's death." And we see at the end: "Six weeks after this adventure, my father was stricken by an abcess . . . , which carried him off in eight days." It would obviously be tempting to see a link between this death and Casanova's dirty trick. His father's anger could well have gone to the stalwart man's head and turned into a deadly abcess. Indeed, the incident unfolds as if Casanova had heard our silly interpretation and was mocking us along with all of the respectable physicians of his day: it was not I who killed him; it was those charlatans who came to treat him. One must listen carefully to the mocking tone he assumes in scoffing at the authority of the medical profession, for it determines the rest of the story:

Doctor Zambelli first gave him oppilative remedies, and seeing his mistake, he tried to correct it by administering castoreum [an antispasmodic], which sent his patient into convulsions and killed him. The abcess burst through the ear a minute after his death; it left as soon as it killed him, as if it had no more business there. My father, only thirty-six years old, was in the prime of life when he died. His death was mourned by the public, particularly by the Venetian nobility, who considered him superior to his profession as much for his conduct as for his knowledge of mechanics. Two days before his death, he gathered his children around his bed, along with his wife and three Venetian noblemen named Grimani whose protection he wished to entreat in our favor.   (1: 7–8)

We should note, in passing, the presence of these Grimani, for we shall meet them again.

If, therefore, this episode were to be read against the backdrop of his father's death, Casanova, as usual, would inform us that he had nothing to do with it. As for rivalry, the key to Casanova's game is not to bother with it. Although he may have provoked his father's anger, he is not about to suffer the consequences—he diverts his father's wrath onto his brother. Here again, as with Razzetta and as in the seminary, the guilty party seems to be innocent and the innocent party guilty. This results in a false confrontation through which the two protagonists—the father and the brother—are ridiculed without even realizing it. Death has nothing to do with the son's desire for murder and his consequential guilt; likewise, the rivalry between father and son bears no relation to their actions and therefore functions only to entertain the person who staged the scene and the spectators who read it.

Casanova's invocation of the story of Jacob and Esau serves a similar function: it reshuffles the cards so that no one can draw any conclusions from the incident. Casanova does not supplant his older brother, for he is the older brother; hence he has given up his place both as firstborn son and as guilty brother in order to pass it on to his brother. Yet it is a different rule that emerges as the key to Casanova's game. In fact, this story is situated not only between two mentions of his father's death, but also between his father's work on optics and the figure of Israel the seer. Moreover, the stolen object is no mere trifle. It is a finely faceted crystal that captivates one's gaze when held up to the eyes. Casanova's whole life will be marked by his attempt to transport reality to the footlights of the stage. His primary goal is to expose everything, not only by creating a whirlwind of seductions, games, and journeys, but also by brutally exposing all of the usually well-kept secrets. Like a brilliant multifaceted crystal, the *Memoirs* illuminate the inner state of Casanova and of all his protagonists; for everything must be seen and brought to light. As he writes at the end of chapter 7, on the subject of women, without the sparkle of appearance, nothing is left.

According to the subtitle of a book by Félicien Marceau, Casanova is the anti–Don Juan.* And, in his lighthearted way, he took great pains to be just that. For an anti–Don Juan must avoid grandiloquence under all circumstances and guard carefully against the threat that life might surreptitiously become history. He must instead ensure that life remains a series of adventures determined only by the whim of fortune; that reality not become substantial, but rather that it always be mastered by the imagination; that guilt be no more than a minor hindrance, shaken off with a good night's sleep. For Casanova, the ultimate goal of social ties is not love or sacrifice, but the generalized laughter that allows the laugher to remain blind to himself even while it unmasks every face, including his own. Surely no one has gone farther than Casanova in the quest to express himself, for he does not spare himself in his self-portrayal; yet he can pursue this undertaking only through constant evasion and the never-ending role-playing characteristic of an actor.

We nonetheless have the right to wonder about the origins of this singular character who is always so eager to undo the basic foundations of society, usually under the guise of remaining true to the highest principles. Here is what J. Rives Childs—one of the most eminent specialists on the Venetian's biography—tells us on this question: "Casanova's acknowledged father was Gaëtan Joseph Jacques, of Parma. . . . While playing at the Grimani's S. Samuele Theatre in Venice, he married February 27, 1724, the daughter of a shoe-

---

* *Casanova ou l'anti–Don Juan* (Gallimard, 1948).

maker, Zanetta Farussi, whom he introduced in turn to the stage."
And he goes on:

The genealogy Casanova offers of his paternal line, however doubtful may
be its integral authenticity, is interesting as containing some of the seeds of
his own career. There are strong reasons for believing, however, that he
may not have been the son of Gaëtan but the issue of the Venetian patrician
Michel Grimani, whose brother, Abbé Alvise Grimani, became Casanova's
guardian. In the *Commediante in fortuna* (1755), Abbé Chiari represented
Casanova as a bastard, while he himself in *Né Amori, Né Donne*, written in
1782, ascribed his origin to Michel Grimani.*

Hence the legal father, Gaëtan Casanova, may not be the biologi-
cal father of our memoirist. We can understand from this bit of
information why the Grimani brothers were present at Gaëtan Casanova's deathbed along with the family; we can also see why it is
the Abbé Alvise Grimani, and not his brother Michel, who becomes Giacomo Casanova's tutor, for such a position would have
designated Michel too obviously as the boy's noble progenitor. Finally, we understand why Casanova was thrilled to settle the score
as soon as possible with this Abbé Grimani through the hapless
mediator Razzetta, for he could get back at the abbé's brother
Michel in the process. After all, Casanova's passion for abolishing
secrets could well have its source in the secret that was imposed
upon him from the beginning. It is not unreasonable to suppose
that the fact of being a bastard, which everyone knew without
acknowledging it, could have had some effect on the destiny of
Jacques Casanova. Yet, since all bastards do not share the same obsessive passion for revenge, we shall have to conclude that this detail
does not prove anything—except that one swallow does not make
the springtime, and that a parameter should not be taken for a cause
any more than a model should be used as a universal explanation.

* *Casanova: A Biography Based on New Documents* (London: Allen and Unwin,
1961), pp. 30–32.

The Passage into Horror

CASANOVA'S endless adventures do not deter him from realizing the plans that his mother had made for him. Thanks to the monk whom she had met in Warsaw and for whom she obtains a bishopric in Calabria, the young abbé should soon be "on his way to the highest offices of the Church" (1: 116). Thus Casanova is told to travel to Calabria—to Martirano (he writes Martorano) to be exact—via Rome and Naples. The tale of this strange voyage, recounted in chapter 8 of the first volume, provides illuminating details that, far from minimizing the misery and abjection of the journey, actually accentuate its sordid elements. This voyage represents Casanova's true initiation as a libertine and serves as evidence that he could not avoid passing through horror in his quest to attain the highest degree of derision possible.

The chapter opens on Casanova's woeful mishaps in Chioggia, a small port not far from Venice, where the boat that is transporting him to Ancona makes a stop. From the third day on, he finds himself in the dubious company of a debauched monk, who leads him into whorehouses and gambling joints. Result: a woman leaves him with a stingingly painful souvenir, and he loses all of his money playing faro.* As if that were not enough, Casanova is invited the next day by Corsini, the monk, to make up his loss. To do so, he pawns the contents of his trunk, all that remains of his

---

*Faro was a popular card game in Casanova's day.

possessions. He gets thirty sequins for it,* and breaks his bank that very night.

Casanova's multiple bankruptcies plunge him into the deepest of sleeps, what he calls "the brother of death" (1: 163)—a death wish:

> I went to bed stunned. I awoke after eleven hours of heavy sleep, but my heart was so heavy that I simply stayed in bed. In my wretched state I found all thought abhorrent and could not face the light of day, for I felt myself unworthy of it. I dreaded rousing myself entirely, knowing that I would then have to face the cruel necessity of making some decision. . . . I was weary of my existence, and I entertained some vague hope of starving to death where I was without leaving my bed. It is certain that I should not have gotten up if M. Alban, the master of the tartan,† had not roused me by shaking me out of my stupor and informing me that I should board the boat, for the wind was good and he wanted to leave. (1: 164–65)

What is emphasized in this passage are the traits that define a libertine initiation: loss of sexual capacity, of earthly goods, and of life. But, obviously, this triple loss does not in itself suffice to set him off on a libertine career, so a touch of the sordid must be added: not only is he afflicted by a venereal disease, but he has contracted it from a "miserable ugly slut" (1: 163). His pockets are empty not only from gambling, but from gambling with thieves in a seedy dive. Finally, Casanova yearns to die, not out of bravado, but out of fear of "rousing myself entirely" and then having to "mak[e] some decision."

For these are the requirements Casanova must satisfy in order to succeed in his endeavor: he must never have anything to do with what happens to him. To be more precise, Casanova's libertine strategy must be carried out in a fatal state of powerlessness. And yet, in truth, Casanova knows very well what he is getting himself into:

> The young doctor [whom he had met the first day of his arrival in Chioggia] made another friendly gesture: he forewarned me that the monk Corsini was a very worthless fellow, despised by everybody, and advised me to avoid him. I thanked the good doctor for the information; but I didn't take it seriously, because I believed that Corsini's bad reputation stemmed

---

*A sequin was a type of gold coin first used in Venice around the end of the thirteenth century.

†A small, single-masted Mediterranean ship.

only from his being a libertine. Of a tolerant disposition, and too giddy to fear any snares, I thought that the monk would, on the contrary, provide me with plenty of entertainment. (1: 162–63)

It is undoubtedly Casanova's desire for "entertainment" that leads him on, yet he cannot obtain such pleasures without ceding his initiative, without submitting to someone else, like a victim of destiny. He goes on: "On the third day, the fatal monk took me into a place that I could have entered on my own." Translated into our terms: since I could *not* have gone there on my own, welcome is the monk who turns my decision to follow him into a necessity. Casanova later uses the term "sacred executioner" (1: 163) to designate Corsini, an indication that he considers himself the victim of a holocaustic force, the helpless pawn of fate. Just as Casanova's elaborate stagings of his intrigues with women are meant to foster misprision and willful ignorance of sexual and personal identity, so, too, his libertine aims must be converted into a form of behavior blind to its own actions.

It is in this optimal condition that Casanova leaves Chioggia and returns, after a difficult sea passage, to Orsana, a small port on the Istrian Peninsula, where he is invited to travel with another monk, Friar Steffano:

I had not eaten a thing for thirty-six hours, and having suffered much from seasickness during the night, I had thrown up whatever was still left in my stomach. In addition, my secret illness made me exceedingly uncomfortable, and my mind was heavily burdened by my wretched situation, for I had not a cent to my name. *I was in such a miserable state that I lacked the strength to have a desire of any kind.* I followed the monk in absolute apathy. (1: 165–66)

It is Casanova's own hand that underscores the sentence shown here in italics. We see him here at the outer reaches of his humanity: he has gone beyond banal irresponsibility or a mere inability to choose, to take a stand, to decide; he has come to the limits of indistinction, the point of dissolution of the self—in a word, a state in which he is utterly incapable of establishing his identity, of saying yes or no to anything, "lack[ing] the strength to have a desire of any kind."

We should not take this sentence lightly, as if it were describing a mere passing mood. For Casanova's present condition is the perfect incarnation of the precept M. Malipiero had taught him just after his grandmother's death, when Casanova was enthusiastically dreaming of leaving Venice in order to "fulfill [his] destiny elsewhere" (1: 117): "Give yourself up to whatever fate offers you, provided you do not feel an invincible repugnance to accepting it." We shall hear the echo of this precept several times in this tale. When Steffano reappears in the nick of time to save Casanova from great distress, Casanova exclaims: "Whether it was heaven or hell that sent him to me, I saw that I had to submit to him. He was to escort me to Rome—it was destiny's decree" (1: 185). And shortly afterward, he says in a similar vein: "I resigned myself to my destiny and went with him to Soma" (1: 188).

It is hardly arbitrary that a monk should serve as Casanova's instrument of destiny, or that he should pass from the hands of Corsini—"a Jacobin friar, blind in one eye, from Modena" (1: 162)—into the grips of Steffano, "a young monk of the order of the Recollets" (1: 162), who plunges the young abbé into the sordid even as he pulls him out of it. One could conclude that Casanova lets himself be taken in by people of this ilk because he is preparing for an ecclesiastic career and finds them natural companions; but in fact he has some scores to settle with characters who resemble him too closely, characters from whom he must distinguish himself. Each time he succeeds in leaving Steffano in the midst of their travels from Ancona to Rome, Casanova finds him again, by chance, a few miles down the road. Their paths diverge and cross just as their personas do. Like Casanova, Steffano is poor, but he knows how to beg in the name of Saint Francis and is diabolically successful at it: "It occurred to me that what this monk called wealth consisted precisely in what I considered the source of my misery" (1: 168). For Casanova, lacking money is an unbearable "abasement"; he admires Steffano for using his poverty to such profit. (But is Steffano so different from the character who will later exploit the gullibility of zealots of cabalistic and alchemical practices in hopes of swindling them?) Steffano does not want to work and shuffles along the road begging out of laziness; but Casanova will choose not to work either, probably out of the ethical conviction that chance alone (and perhaps a few expedients) should nourish him. The monk "had no taste whatever for women, nor for any other pleasure of the flesh." Yet he wallows in licentiousness: "On that score he considered everything fair game for merriment; and when he had drunk too much, he would ask his tablemates—husbands, wives, sons, and daughters—such lewd questions that they would all blush. The brute would only laugh at them" (1: 181). But Casanova, who has a notably strong taste for women, takes them seriously only in order to dispense with them that much faster. Whereas Steffano passes himself off as a priest, insolently conducts mass, hears confession, and even refuses to absolve a nice girl, Casanova (who defends her) is an exemplary pilgrim, making a detour through Loreto to visit "the very house where the Blessed Virgin gave birth to her Creator" (1: 179). Casanova must hide the fact (from himself above all) that he is just as cynical as his friend the monk. Yet he knows full well that the two of them have much in common.

The abbé and the monk embark on a voyage that is riddled with disputes and ruptures, a progressive march toward ignominy— every separation (there are three in all) is an attempt to break off complicitous situations, each more serious than the previous. Steffano first compromises Casanova by making him write letters full of "lies" (1: 170) in order to have provisions sent to them during their quarantine in Ancona. Casanova puts up a weak defense before the threat of having nothing more to eat. During this period, he begins an intrigue with a Greek slave woman (1: 171–76) and parts with his monk to make an apparently sincere pilgrimage to Loreto. After their second encounter, Steffano compromises the abbé by pretending to be a priest; although Casanova protests (mostly in private), he refrains from unmasking his companion (1: 181). Casanova pays for his effort to keep away from this scoundrel—out of a fear of "seeing myself condemned to the galleys with him" (1: 181)—by losing his purse, wounding his leg, and spending a night with other scoundrels, that is, with *sbires*, a coarse breed of Italian soldiers whom he calls "those cursed enemies of the human race" (1: 183). Whether he distances himself or approaches Steffano, Casanova follows the same, steady descent into sordidness. When he meets up with the monk a third time, Steffano gets Casanova out of a dangerous fix, only to plunge him further into abasement than before. Soon after arriving at a miserable hut, they are robbed, Casanova is almost raped by one of the "wretched females" who had received them, and

Steffano kills an old man with his staff in a midnight brawl (1: 186–87). Steffano the riffraff, Steffano the impostor, Steffano the assassin—this is the triple image that punctuates Casanova's fall into the lowest depths.

Another comically grotesque episode confirms the guarded proximity of the two men. As Casanova recounts, one day "he told me that he would walk twice as far as usual, if I agreed to carry his cloak, which he found quite heavy. I was willing to try, and so he put on my topcoat. We looked like two comic characters and made every passerby laugh. His cloak was in fact heavy enough to burden a mule" (1: 179–80). Something decisive is at stake for Casanova in this exchange of clothing. This journey supposes that the proximity between the two travelers is unveiled, but it also assumes that it is resolved. By taking up with Corsini and then with Steffano, Casanova seeks to rid himself of religion by subjecting it to constant derision. Clearly, it is his companion of the moment who is to carry out this task, while Casanova plays the role of the honest believer. The sluggard, the rogue, the impostor—the three constitute the negative, revealing side of respectable religion (the kind of religion whose naïve followers pop up "at every turn of the road"; 1: 180), which knows how to transform happenstance into Providence, pronounce immutable laws, and ensure that everyone obeys them. Steffano's pace is neither too fast nor too slow, he is in perfect health, and nothing bad ever happens to him (1: 185). To tell the truth, nothing at all ever happens to him over the course of his endlessly repetitive days. Steffano represents Casanova's temptation, an ecclesiastic career in which stability wins out over hypocrisy. Casanova might have succeeded at such a career, but to do so, he would have been obliged to take his destiny in hand rather than submitting to it; he would have had to plan his success one step at a time rather than waiting for success to come with a roll of the die. If Casanova detests the proximity of Steffano—a man he obviously admires, for he goes so far as to imitate him, "boldly going out begging for food, just as Friar Steffano had taught me" (1: 190)—it is not because this man is a coarse ignoramus, but because he so attracts Casanova. Steffano knows how to travel across the world without lacking for anything essential; he can use the gullibility of others to get himself a good meal; his rather heavy-handed cunning shields him from day-to-day uncertainties; and the poverty that he has transformed into his greatest source of wealth protects him forever from happenstance.

It is precisely happenstance that Casanova wants to make into his religion—a constant sense of the unexpected by which life seems an eternal beginning that never develops, the incomprehensible sense of being caught unawares that exempts one both from any understanding of the events taking place and from any attempt to control them. Steffano's laziness is supported by an economic and religious system in which he functions as an experienced profiteer; in contrast, Casanova defies the order of events by constantly appealing to the extraordinary. Casanova leaves Friar Steffano and sets out on his own, only to injure his foot, lose all his money, and end up penniless before a surgeon and an innkeeper who demand to be paid:

I must ask my reader whether it is possible, in the face of such extraordinary circumstances, not to yield to superstition? What is most amazing in this case is the precise minute at which the event occurred, for the monk arrived at the very last; and what surprised me even more was the force of Providence, of Fortune, of whatever necessary combination it was that willed, ordained, compelled me, to find no hope but in that fatal monk, who had begun to be my protective genius in Chioggia at the beginning of my travails. But what a guardian angel! I could not help looking upon this mysterious force as more of a punishment than a favor. Yet I was greatly relieved to see this dumb, shifty, uneducated scoundrel, for I did not for a minute doubt that he would get me out of my difficulties. Whether it was heaven or hell that sent him to me, I saw that I had to submit to him. He was to escort me to Rome—it was destiny's decree. (1: 184–85)

Casanova would undoubtedly place this pseudo-fortuitous meeting in the same category of phenomena as the flash of light that appears before him on the road:

An hour after I had left Castelnuovo on my way to Rome, the atmosphere being calm and the sky clear, I perceived on my right, and within ten paces of me, a pyramidal flame about two feet long and four or five feet above the ground, which seemed to be accompanying me. It would stop when I stood still, and when the road along which I was traveling happened to be lined with trees, I no longer saw it, but it was sure to reappear as soon as I had passed the trees. . . . What a wonder for superstitious ignorance it would have been if, having had witnesses to that phenomenon, I had made a great fortune in Rome! History is full of such trifles, and the world is full of people who attach great importance to them in spite of the so-called light that the sciences offer the human mind. In truth, I must confess that, although somewhat versed in physics, the sight of that small meteor did not fail to give me singular ideas.   (1: 189–90)

The same young man who claims to be an intellectual light is seized with superstition, for he adores a phenomenon that has no discernible cause, rhyme, or reason, whose appearances and disappearances defy explanation—a phenomenon that abolishes time and makes man, above all, seem an ephemeral fluke, an accident with no future, a purely theatrical image that ceases to exist as soon as the footlights go out, not substantial enough even to be called a dream, for a dream can always recur.

Casanova's system adheres to the realm of miracles, miracles that cannot be reproduced. And although the world around him is full of strange, irreproducible phenomena, Casanova will often strive to appear, in the eyes of those around him, as the producer of such illusions. It is no surprise that this initiation journey comes to a close with the tale of Casanova's mercury ploy, which brings him his first financial success. Soon after the account of Casanova's vision of the flame, we read that he arrives at the palace of Portici and makes the acquaintance of a Greek merchant. After extensive wheeling and dealing, during which our abbé dupes the merchant into believing that he possesses a great secret, Casanova sells him a very expensive formula for increasing mercury a quarter by adding lead and bismuth. The hapless merchant is clearly the victim of a double fraud, for he must pay dearly to obtain both the false secret and the right to sell tampered mercury to other potential buyers. But what excites Casanova, in this instance as in others, is the opportunity to make someone believe in a miracle by claiming to be in league with alchemists. For Casanova, there is an unbroken line connecting chemistry, alchemy, superstition, and magic, and passing through the cabala and astrology.

There is, however, another reason that this episode is so dear to Casanova's heart: it marks his ascent out of misery, thanks to the gullibility and generosity of the Greek merchant:

We parted the best friends in the world. . . . Possessing about one hundred sequins and enjoying good health, I was very proud of my success, in which I could not see any cause to reproach myself. The quick-witted cunning that I had used to ensure the sale of my secret could not be faulted except by a kind of morality that has no place in matters of business. In any event, free, rich, and certain of presenting myself before the bishop as a handsome young man, and not like a beggar, I soon recovered my natural spirits and congratulated myself for having gained enough experience, at my own expense, to defend myself against the Friar Corsinis of the world, against thieving gamblers, mercenary women, and particularly those who praise so well the victims they intend to dupe.   (1: 196–97)

By alluding here to the triple loss that had opened the chapter, Casanova accentuates the reversal that has occurred. The reversal is all the more dramatic because it refers us back to the final lines of the preceding chapter, when none of these misadventures could be foreseen, and when the money in his pocket was also the key to his happiness:

M. Grimani had given me ten sequins, which he thought would be more than enough to keep me during the entire time that I was to stay in the lazaretto of Ancona for the necessary quarantine. After that period, it was not to be supposed that I could want any money. Since these gentlemen seemed so certain about the matter, I was bound to defer to their opinion; but in fact I thought little about it. Yet I must say that I found it a great consolation to have, unbeknownst to everybody, forty bright sequins in my purse, which powerfully contributed to my youthful cheerfulness. I left Venice full of joy and without one regret.   (1: 160)

Unlike other memoirists (for example, the anonymous gentleman who wrote *My Secret Life*), Casanova is never boring; for like the author of a gripping potboiler, he knows how to move us, in a single chapter or a sequence of two or three, from laughter to tears and from sadness to hope, by tempering the weight of his misfortunes with sentimental or comic episodes, as in the description offered in this chapter of his aborted encounter with the Greek slave woman who lives one floor below him in the lazaretto, with whom he communicates via a hole in the floor (1: 171–76). The intertwining of moments of great happiness and of failure revealed by the tale reflect the complexity of a character who always has two irons in the fire, and who knows how to strike a subtle mix of sweet and bitter ingredients.

Would Casanova enthrall us so if he had never known chagrin and darkness, if he were not constantly obliged to lift himself up out of the horror and dereliction he had known? Casanova's life is filled with extreme vexations, and his sad end is prepared long in advance. The bit of misery that he presents in this chapter—and that only rarely attracts critical notice—is without any doubt an essential component of his love life. We would like to think that Casanova's sole means of seduction are stature, beauty, and intelligence. Yet Casanova is never able to resist women's tears, because he empathizes with their state of abandonment and is well acquainted himself with chagrin and its peculiar delights. He seduces women because he shares their feeling that everything is futile, their conviction that human existence is founded solely upon failure. The only form of success that Casanova ever tolerated in his life, because he had fervently yearned for it himself, is the success of glittering in the public eye, which women resort to in order to save themselves from the infinite burden of desolation. The secret of seducing women lies in taking part in each woman's woes while lightening part of her burden. If Casanova is seductive in his glitter and finery, it is because the vanity of his appearance both accentuates and effaces the vanity of existence. He knows, as only women can know, that neither work nor power can cure the gloom of existence, and he knows how to laugh along with them.

Casanova is original because, though he may hover near the abyss of the truly sordid, he does not remain there; and when he finds himself dragged down to such a point, he does not lament his fate. He grasps at all possible means, all available resources (even the most derisive), to resist his fascination with this abyss, and he manages to back off from it by the sheer force of his youth and cunning. He also resists through amusement, for he wants to laugh and make his readers laugh, and knows full well that laughter lasts only if it is sustained and justified by the threat of the most dire of possibilities imaginable.

The Irresponsible Runaway

It hardly comes as a surprise that the following chapter, whose tone will be quite different, opens by evoking both tears and laughter. Upon arriving in Naples, Casanova is referred to one Don Gennaro:

> I had no difficulty in answering the many questions that he addressed to me, but I found most singular and extraordinary the continual bursts of laughter that issued forth from his chest with each of my answers. My descriptions of piteous Calabria and of the sad situation of the bishop of Martorano, which I considered more suited to bring tears to a listener's eyes, prompted such violent laughter that I feared it would kill him.
>
> This man was big, fat, and ruddy. Suspecting that he was making fun of me, I was very near getting angry when, calmer at last, he told me with feeling that I must excuse his laughter, which was caused by a disease common in his family, for one of his uncles had died of it.
>
> "He died of laughing?"
>
> "Yes. This disease, which was not known to Hippocrates, is called *li flati.*"
>
> "What? You mean to say that a hypochondriac affection, which makes all of its victims morose, makes you giddy?"   (1: 202)

Obviously, this anecdote does not appear here purely by chance. Rather, it serves as a means for Casanova to announce that he has turned his back on all that might inspire pity and that, from this point on, he will depend solely on laughter, even at the risk of death—in other words, from this point on, his laughter will always be founded upon misery and death.

These brief pages of introduction to his journey from Naples to Rome are a masterpiece of composition. They are marked not only by an accent on Don Gennaro's uncontrollable laughter, but also by an encounter with one Don Antonio Casanova that provides our storyteller with an occasion to fabricate a new account of his own birth, a new genealogy that would have him descend from an illustrious Spaniard. Casanova cleverly reminds us of his recent, painful adventures by combining a description of his reunion with the Greek merchant he had duped a few days earlier (with whom he is on the best of terms) with an astute placement of the following paragraph—immediately after the six pages that relate Don Gennaro's laughing fits and Don Antonio's largesse, and just before the tale of his departure for Rome:

> From my landing in Chioggia up to my arrival in Naples, fortune had treated me unfairly. It was in Naples that I began to breathe more easily; and Naples has always been a fortunate place for me, as my reader will see in the latter part of these *Memoirs*. It was in Portici that I faced that awful moment when my spirit was about to sink into degradation, and *there is no remedy against the degradation of the mind*, for nothing can restore it to its former state. It is a disheartening condition for which there is no possible cure. With his letter to Don Gennaro, the bishop of Martorano corrected all of the wrong that he had done me. I waited until I was in Rome to write to him. (1: 208)

Hence, in the space of a few sentences, Casanova recites the names of all the cities in his past and future. He speaks of Rome, where he is heading, and Naples, where he will meet both Donna Lucrezia (who plays a central role in the next adventure) and the duke of Matalona, whom he had just mentioned (1: 206). But above all, he wants to remind the reader of both Chioggia, where he had lost everything, and Portici, where his good fortune returned. He also wants to remind his audience that, in striking out once again in life, he has risen out of the lowest depths of abasement. For the two chapters (chaps. 9 and 10) that conclude the first volume will also present a mixture of happiness and dashed hopes.

The impatient reader, undoubtedly more impatient than Casanova himself, will find little of interest in these pages beyond the mischievous, comical, happy love story with Donna Lucrezia. Such a reader will overlook the rest, which is nonetheless indispensable to the tale. For, even when enjoying his greatest success, Casanova cannot keep himself from unconsciously preparing some plot that will force him once more to take flight.

While traveling in a coach from Naples to Rome, he makes the acquaintance of a man and two young women, sisters, one of whom is the man's wife. Every stop along the road, where the four travelers sleep in the same room, is an opportunity for Casanova to try to make his way into the bed shared by the two sisters; and the wife, Donna Lucrezia, gladly accepts his advances. Nothing decisive has yet occurred when they arrive in Rome. It is only during later outings in the countryside—first in a carriage and then in wooded groves and meadows—that Casanova enjoys all of Lucrezia's favors. But, because her husband is a lawyer who has come to Rome only in order to plead a case, Lucrezia must return to Naples after a few weeks.

As we see here, Casanova remains true to his phantasms: once again, he needs two sisters in order to fall in love. The schema is slightly modified because the two sisters do not receive his attentions with equal enthusiasm. Whereas Donna Lucrezia falls in love with the young abbé and seeks out any possible occasion to see him, Donna Angelica pretends to resist him; but Angelica is nonetheless a direct witness to their lovemaking. In fact, after spending a rapturous night in the arms of the first sister, Casanova ends up in the embrace of the second. Throughout that night, "she [Angelica] had not slept a minute" (1: 250), remaining ever attentive, curious, and active after her own fashion. There is more expressed in her exclamation to Casanova—"No, I do not hate you"—than a simple regret at having waited so long to give herself to him.

This is an inverted proof of Casanova's need to have two sisters at the same time. When Lucrezia is about to leave, she whispers this to him: "I have enlightened my sister. Instead of pitying me, she must now heartily approve of my actions, she must surely love you; since I am about to leave, I leave her to you" (1: 252). For Angelica is staying in Rome, where she is to be married in a few weeks. It would have been easy for Casanova to continue to court her and arrange romantic trysts. But he declines Lucrezia's suggestion and goes so far as to say that "he must take care not to upset the peace of happy households" (1: 252). It is true, lest we forget, that we have before us a champion of every possible category of honest morality. Casanova's unconscious is one of his most precious gifts, and nothing could deprive him of it. For, in the end, the whole adventure with Donna Lucrezia takes place under the blind eye of their unknowing accomplice, Lucrezia's lawyer husband. We can even confidently assert that this is another necessary ingredient in Casanova's romantic escapades, and in the risks he repeatedly takes to make his way into Lucrezia's bed or to get her to travel with him in his carriage or in his berlin, an enclosed two-seater that was called at the time a *vis-à-vis*.

Donna Lucrezia has everything necessary to attract our young abbé, and I refer not to her physical charms, undoubtedly incontestable, but to her situation. She is "just passing through" in three respects: she is married and thus belongs to another man, and has neither any intention nor any possibility of leaving him; her stay in Rome is guaranteed to be brief, since her husband is only there on business; and the lovers are forced to meet for their trysts in carriages, in post houses, and on promenades in the country. Donna Lucrezia perfectly fits the tropes according to which Casanova's love affairs are played out: she embodies brevity, haste, furtive happiness, and the banishment of any tragic element. * After her departure, Casanova complains not of sadness or heartbreak, but of boredom (1: 253); she was only a passing thrill, so there is no wound left by her absence.

We should, however, take care in reading Casanova's message: love is not what allows him to pass the time, but rather the means he employs to make time pass. In order to overcome boredom, most men try to fill their days by modifying the things or relations around them; they root themselves in the temporal and, in the process, some grow up, while others simply grow hard or rotten. They usually sink into dejection or melancholy, having realized that time has gotten the better of them. This will happen one day to our young lover, but for the time being, he adopts the tactic of denying

---

*On Casanova's relationship to time, see Georges Poulet's remarkable study *Mesure de l'instant*, vol. 4 of *Etudes sur le temps humain* (Librairie Plon, 1968), pp. 105–40.

time by reducing it to successive flashes, to impromptu appearances, to bursts that are both violent and fleeting. Each of Casanova's love affairs must be a beginning that never develops into anything and, hence, has no end.

Donna Lucrezia is just passing through, and for Casanova this is a necessary condition of his love for her. But because that is not enough for him, he arranges circumstances so that he too is merely passing through Rome. The *day after* he wins Lucrezia's affections completely—the timing is worth remarking—he introduces onto the scene Barbaruccia, the pretty girl who, through the mediation of her fiancé, will cause Casanova's expulsion from the city (1: 230). He could have mentioned her earlier, for they had already met; but after the first sexual union that threatens to get him involved, the presence of this girl is literarily indispensable for Casanova to begin his retreat and prepare his escape.

The story surrounding Barbaruccia had started quietly. Casanova had all the makings of a perfect secretary, all that is necessary to embark on an ecclesiastic career in Rome. The only thorny question that he is asked by Father Georgi, to whom he was referred, concerns his knowledge of French (1: 218). The question becomes an order when he meets Cardinal Acquaviva: "You must apply yourself quickly to the study of French; it is indispensable" (1: 220). Until he "learns the French language," Casanova will have nothing to do but make "extracts from letters" (1: 222). So Casanova is to learn French (1: 225, 227), and it is this unfortunate detail, this trivial fault, that brings about his undoing, because his language instructor is Barbaruccia's father.

After introducing us to Barbaruccia, Casanova relates that she is in love with a young man who had been thrown out by her father after he had "caught them at five in the morning in a situation that declared [them] to be guilty lovers" (1: 231). The young man comes to see our abbé to bemoan his situation, and Casanova accepts or feels forced to help him by acting as a mediator between the two lovers. Casanova knows full well that he should not get even the slightest bit mixed up in this business, yet he nonetheless lets himself be dragged into it little by little.

From the beginning of these chapters, Casanova has prepared us to see him stumble into this misadventure. For example, immedi-

47

ately after the mention of his arrival in Rome, he makes the follow-ing declaration and takes care to underscore it, as if he were pre-senting a program that he had to carry out:

> Rome was the one city in which a man had often started with nothing and risen to great heights, and it should surprise no one that I believed I had all of the requisite qualities. The full purse in my pocket so increased my self-confidence that it knew no bounds, and my inexperience prevented me from checking this unbridled opinion of my abilities.
>
> The man who intends to make his fortune in this ancient capital must be a chameleon who can take on all the colors reflected in the atmosphere that surrounds him. . . . If, unfortunately, he is not religious at heart, he must be religious in his mind; if he is an honest man, he must suffer quietly the mortifying knowledge that he is a hypocrite. If he loathes such a fiction, he should leave Rome and go to seek his fortune in England. I do not know whether I am boasting or excusing myself, but out of all these necessary qualities, I possessed none save for an accommodating disposition, which, in isolation, is a fault. I was an interesting, heedless fellow, a fairly hand-some horse from a good bloodline, but not broken, or, rather, badly bro-ken, which is even worse.   (1: 217)

In counterpoint to this warning, given to the reader as a pre-lude to Casanova's stay in Rome, there appears a few pages later another warning—also underscored—formulated by his mentor, Father Georgi: "'Remember,' this wise man told me, 'that to lead a blameless life you must curb your passions, and that whatever mis-fortune may befall you, no one will attribute it to bad luck or fate, for these words are meaningless; all of the fault will fall on your head'" (1: 223).

Hence we have a description of each blade of the steel trap that is about to close on Casanova: on the one hand, his interesting heed-lessness, that is, his engaging irresponsibility; and on the other hand, the inevitable responsibility that falls to him. In Rome, you are responsible not only for your actions, but also for every-thing that befalls you. The city is therefore not suitable for Casa-nova, for neither good nor bad fortune is recognized there, only facts and their real or supposed agents. But this city is also a stroke of luck for the author of these *Memoirs*, for it allows him to paint himself as a victim of circumstance, a victim who always seems lucid, but who is honestly incapable of acting in any other fashion.

From his very first encounter with Barbaruccia's lover, who tells him the tale of his woes, Casanova knows that he should stay out of this intrigue: "I could do nothing but pity him, for in the name of honor I could not interfere in such a business." Yet a few moments later, he reverses his stance: "We were on the quay of Rippeta, and when I observed that he was casting dark looks toward the Tiber, I feared his despair might lead him to do something suicidal, so I promised to make some inquiries about Barbaruccia from her father and to inform him of all I heard" (1: 231–32).

The same dance of hesitation, between his refusal to help the young lovers and the impossibility of avoiding it, continues:

The next day, after having received my lesson from M. Dalacqua, I was going down the stairs on my way out when I saw Barbaruccia, who, while passing from one room to another, dropped a letter and earnestly looked at me. I felt bound to pick it up, because the servant who was coming up the stairs would have seen it. The letter, which enclosed another, said this: "If you think that it would be wrong to give this letter to your friend, burn it. Have pity on a miserable soul and be discreet." (1: 232–33)

Although he may have been bound to pick up the letter, he is not obliged to pass on the one enclosed. He decides therefore to return it to the girl, adding a note to explain that he cannot "do her this minor service." This noble act goes unaccomplished. Casanova writes his note that evening and puts the letter in his pocket: "The next day, I went to return the letter to her, but because I had changed my trousers, I could not find it; since I had obviously left it in my room, I had to postpone the delivery until the next day. Besides, I did not see the girl" (1: 233). This is indeed a curious double way of clearing himself of blame. He not only forgets the letter (one certainly has the right to change one's pants), but would have been unable to give it to her even if he had not forgotten it. The unlucky Casanova truly has nothing to do with any of this and can do nothing to help.

Predictably, the poor devastated young man comes to Casanova's room that evening and "declares his despair": "He spoke of killing himself because he believed deep down that Barbaruccia had decided to forget him. I could think of no other way to persuade him that this notion was false than to give him the letter. This was my first mistake in this fatal affair, a mistake committed out of softheartedness" (1: 233). So Casanova knows that he has made a mistake: "I should not have agreed to play Mercury in this affair. To avoid getting involved, I needed only to recall that Father Georgi certainly would never have approved of my accommodating disposition" (1: 234). What reappears here is the "accommodating disposition" that he had singled out upon arriving in Rome as his unique quality, a quality that becomes a fault in isolation. Casanova nonetheless continues to serve both parties, transmitting letters from one to the other: "I ceased to interfere in this intrigue, for I saw quite clearly the dire consequences that could result from it; but the damage was already done" (1: 242).

Of course, the dire consequences arrive. Barbaruccia is pregnant and devises a plan to run away with her lover. The attempt fails, the young man is arrested, and the girl seeks refuge in Casanova's room. Even now he knows what course he should take but does not:

> Recognizing Barbaruccia, I close my door; I guess what had happened, and, foreseeing the consequences, know that I am done for. Troubled and muddleheaded, I do not bother to ask her any questions or mince words: I scold her for having chosen my room as a hideout and beg her to leave.
>
> Miserable fool! I should not have begged her, but instead forced her, and even called for help should she refuse to go. But I did not have the strength.
>
> At the mere mention of leaving, she throws herself at my feet crying, moaning, and beseeching me to take pity on her. I gave in, but warned her that we were both done for. (1: 267)

Accommodating as always. But he cannot resist a woman's tears:

> But, when I said these last words, she began to shed such tears that I hardly know how to describe them. I understood how frightful her situation must have been and realized that it was much worse than my own; but that did not ease my sense that this was the eve of my downfall, innocent as I was. (1: 268)

Then he waxes lyrical: "Do you know, dear reader, how powerful such tears can be, flowing from the eyes of a young, pretty girl, honest in character and *unhappy*? Their force is irresistible. I found myself physically incapable of throwing her out" (1: 268–69).

These are indeed fitting words for portraying Casanova: he is innocent because he is in the grip of an irresistible force, because he is physically incapable of resisting. If he is irresponsible, it is not because he was never called upon to act responsibly, but rather because he is the pawn of fortune. To bring an end to this intrigue (of which he is considered "the instigator" by the people of Rome; 1: 275), Casanova has the cardinal, his protector, dismiss the young abbé with a pronouncement that ensures that, once again, Casanova is an innocent victim—to be more precise, a man of honor who is condemned because he could not commit treason. This page is worth citing in its entirety, so well does it reveal the double figure of this character:

> The affair of the Dalacqua girl is finished, and no one even speaks of it anymore; but, without accusing us of scandal-mongering, the public has decided that you and I took advantage of the young man's blunder. They can talk all they want, for if a similar case arose, I would behave no differently; and I do not care to know what no one can force you to say, indeed, what you should not say as a man of honor. If you had known nothing in advance, you would have committed a barbarous, even cowardly act in ordering the girl out of your room, an act that would have left her unhappy for the rest of her days, and left you in any case suspected of complicity and, what is worse, of treason. But despite all of that, you can imagine that, though I disdain all speculations of this sort, I nonetheless cannot help being deeply affected by them. That being the case, I find myself forced to ask you not only to leave me, but to leave Rome; I will, however, provide you with a pretext by which you can save your honor, not to mention the high consideration that you may have obtained through my public expressions of esteem for you. I will allow you to confide to anyone you please, and even announce to everyone, that you are going on a journey to carry out a commission I have given you. (1: 275–76)

Casanova's ill-fated ignorance of French has grown to the dimensions of a state scandal. Although he is not guilty in this matter, he provokes a political scandal that rocks the Vatican itself. He will not pursue the brilliant career that he had imagined in Rome, but his departure for Constantinople as Cardinal Acquaviva's special envoy shows the splendid underside of such a career. His failure—slowly prepared, and faithfully reproduced by the text with fine strokes and successive amplifications—is, finally, a success. The victim is sacrificed upon a theater constructed to his measure.

We must return to the question of the art of composition employed in these chapters. To determine the decisive role played by Casanova's apprenticeship in French, it suffices to note that he mentions it at a point situated between these two chapters. The ninth chapter ends with this sentence: "The next day I went to take my lesson at the usual hour." And the tenth chapter begins: "It was Barbaruccia who gave it to me, because her father was gravely ill." This break, insignificant in appearance, shows clearly that Casanova leaves nothing to chance: the French lesson is indeed the pivot around which the memoirist's destiny turns here. It is amusing to note that Laforgue, who did not understand the storyteller's art, awkwardly translates this as, "Because M. Dalacqua was gravely ill, it was his daughter Barb who gave me the lesson." Casanova had refrained from calling the father by his name here, because the important character in this episode is not Dalacqua, but Barbaruccia.

Through the conjunction of the figures of Lucrezia and Barbaruccia, we find once again the double face that we had met earlier: the woman who enchants Casanova by engaging him in guilt-free transgression, and the woman who causes his downfall even though he is innocent. Casanova does not pay for having transgressed moral or social rules, but solely because he remains faithful to the code of honor. We can attribute Casanova's ease in portraying himself so crudely to the fact that, for the most part, he considered himself to be above reproach. In his own eyes, he does not flee—he is just obliged to leave; it is for this reason that he secretly constructs his downfall on the basis of details he could not control, because they were merely the pitfalls of destiny.

Many critics, readers of Casanova, have refused to see him as anything but a hedonist who is as quick to throw himself into pleasures as he is to retreat from them, so that he can begin them over again. This is undoubtedly true. But this is a hedonist of a singular nature: he can fully savor his pleasures only if he skirts the abyss of the sordid, for *jouissance* contains equal parts of the sordid and the sublime.

A third feminine figure appears in these chapters: Marquise G., the powerful friend of Cardinal S. G. Casanova feels an intense attraction for her, yet it leads to nothing more than a kiss—which he explains by telling us that he ran out of time because he had to leave Rome. This is a false excuse, for he has already given ample proof that he has no need for time in such matters. In truth, Marquise G. is unattainable from the beginning because she is an aloof woman who wants to make love only through the exchange of poems. She is an untouchable, unique woman who opens the path to the multitude of women—another incarnation of Angela, whom he failed to sway, but who directed him to the bed of Marton and Nanette.

Moreover, by her own power and her friendship with a cardinal, this marquise stands out against the backdrop of the rather unsavory politics of Rome, accommodatingly described here. It is a world of chameleons (1: 217), devoid of any rules (1: 219–20), a mixture of depravity (1: 225–26) and treachery (1: 274–75). The putrid ecclesiastic miseries upon which he trod during his initiation journey now writhe under the feet of the haughty marquise. Casanova has not finished making such contrasts, but he has now traced them so vividly that we can no longer detach his image from them.

The Disappearance of the Feminine

CASANOVA has already illustrated several times over that he must not be aware of differences between the sexes or individuals. During his stay in Ancona, on his way from Rome, he stages an extreme demonstration of this refusal to know, and shows us how a passion, or madness, can flare in the face of sexual indeterminacy.

The two chapters that touch upon this brief stay (chapters 1 and 2 of vol. 2) open upon an altercation between Casanova and an innkeeper who refuses to let him break Lent by eating meat, despite Casanova's assurances that he has received a verbal dispensation from the pope. The chapters end with a lost passport and a runaway horse. Because of his refusal to keep Lent, Casanova is able to meet Bellino-Thérèse, the man/woman castrato; in deciding to marry her, he crosses over a (sexual) boundary in spite of himself. His amorous passion is awakened against a backdrop of conceit and is snuffed out when he is forced to take flight.

Casanova is arguing brutishly with the innkeeper when he is interrupted by a solemn man who tells him that he is in the wrong and invites him to come listen to the singing of an actress who is staying in the next room. He finds there "a middle-aged woman who was eating supper with two young girls and two handsome boys" (2: 2). Bellino, the older boy, is a castrato who plays the role of starring actress in the theater of Ancona, and his brother Petrone "had played the principal female dancer." The two sisters are called

Cécile and Marine, "both of them pretty" (2: 3). We are already in a register of sexual ambiguity that was customary in the theatrical world of Casanova's day, for, in many cities, women were not allowed to appear on the stage. The ambiguity increases and becomes fraught with uncertainty when Casanova notes that Bellino's face, like the contours of his chest, seems feminine. But that is not all: Petrone, who is waiting upon Casanova, is a boy prostitute who offers him his services. "I gave him the eighteen paoli left over as a gift, which he accepted with a mark of gratitude designed to make me fully aware of his tastes. He gave me a full, wet kiss on the lips, believing that I, too, was fond of such practices" (2: 4).

This context makes Casanova more flammable than a tinderbox. He embarks on a furious race to confirm his suspicion that Bellino is not a boy. First he bribes the mother, hoping that money will make her talk, but he gets no answer from her except that the castrato had been "inspected" by Monsignor the Bishop's confessor. Then he tries to catch Bellino by surprise, but his prey escapes. Furious, and humiliated by his failed efforts, Casanova "decides to get something for his money from the younger sisters" (2: 6). Unable to come up with something better, he returns to his familiar route: first bribing, then taking advantage of the two sisters. He spends a night with Cécile, and another with Marine. But in between these two nights, a strange promenade with Bellino provides him an opportunity to commit an act of violence by which he regains the upper hand. They are strolling through the port when they decide to board "a Turkish vessel that was to set sail for Alexandria." Hardly have they stepped on board than the first person to appear is the beautiful Greek slave woman whom Casanova had left seven years earlier in the lazaretto of Ancona. Casanova feigns interest in buying something from the Turk, husband of the beauty. The wife gets her husband to leave the room for a moment under the pretext of sending him to search for some merchandise: "She runs and throws her arms around my neck, holds me to her breast and says, 'Here is the moment of Fortune.' Feeling no less courageous than she, I sit down, adjust her on top of me, and in less than a minute I do what her master had never done to her in five years" (2: 9).

An actual encounter, an invented encounter, how are we to know? Whatever it may be, it is a necessary encounter for the adventure at hand, in more than one way. Casanova has the habit of punctuating his stories with allusions to preceding chapters. He does this in order to recall their tone and to mark contrasts. Just as his first meeting with Bellino had provided an occasion to mention chapters 9 and 10 of the first volume ("This creature had several of D. Lucrezia's features, and the manners of Marquise G."; 2: 3), so does the appearance of the Greek woman refer us back to the one enjoyable anecdote of the sordid chapter 8. But this appearance achieves more than that. Because it is inserted in the middle of the chapter, this episode is the pivotal event according to which the respective positions of the personae will change. For Bellino, who still does not want to reveal himself, is present at the scene. It is because of him, and for him, that Casanova so brutally demonstrates his virility: "Throughout this very serious episode, what amused me most was the astonishment of Bellino, absolutely immobile and trembling with fear" (2: 9). We have already seen that, at the very beginning of his love life, Casanova's uncertainty about gender, staged with the help of the sisters Nanette and Marton, was offset by his brutal intercourse with the lovely young newlywed. This was in fact purported to cure her of her fear of lightning. Similarly, Casanova uses the Greek woman here to escape for a moment from the anguish that so torments him.

But the brutish form of this encounter is also intended to intimidate Bellino: "While still on the boat, once he had recovered from his fright, he told me I had shown him a phenomenon that he could not believe to be real but that gave him an odd idea of my character" (2: 9). Casanova wants to shake up Bellino, to unleash in him the violence and madness that possess Casanova himself: "I could have soothed Bellino, and put a stop to his well-founded reasoning, by telling him the whole story [that he had known the Greek woman in the lazaretto]; but then I would not have gotten what I wanted out of my exploit" (2: 10).

Casanova must leave for Rimini, the city to which Bellino, too, is traveling. Casanova suggests a deal: I will take you with me, on the condition that I can satisfy my curiosity. Bellino refuses:

> Upon hearing these words, I felt pushed to the limits of my patience, but I controlled myself, and tried gently to put my hand on the spot that would prove me right or wrong; but he used his own hand to foil my search.

"Take your hand away, my dear Bellino."

"No, absolutely not, for you are in a state that terrifies me. I knew it, and I will never give my consent to such horrors. I am going to send you my sisters."

I held him back and pretended to calm myself; but suddenly, believing that I could surprise him, I thrust my arm down along his backside; with a quick hand I was about to reveal his secret by this route, but he was ready for this trick and got up, fighting off my hand, which did not want to let go, with his own, the same hand with which he covered what he called his shame. It was at this moment that I saw he was a man, and believed that I had penetrated his secret in spite of him. Astonished, angered, mortified, and disgusted, I let him leave. I saw that Bellino was truly a man, but a man worthy of disdain as much for his degradation as for the shameful serenity in which I had observed him during a moment when I should not have seen such clear evidence of his insensitivity.   (2: 14)

Casanova has seen what he sought to see, yet is not satisfied, even though he decides to depart on his journey with the castrato. There now begins a dialogue in which Casanova threatens his companion should he not allow Casanova to verify, by touch, his conviction that he is indeed dealing with a man. Casanova's line of argument is still the same: if I can prove that you are really a man, I will stop loving you and regain my senses. Bellino's reasoning is the opposite, as if he were clearheaded enough to formulate what Casanova does not want to admit to himself: "'You would not be cured,' Bellino answered, with a courage and gentle tone that surprised me, 'for you are in love with me whether I be a girl or a boy, and if you had found that I was a boy, you would have continued to be yourself, and my refusals would have made you even more furious'" (2: 17–18).

Casanova is grappling here with one of the most critical questions of his existence; he allows Bellino to go on speaking at length, for he knows that he has found a first-rate interpreter. The castrato does in fact explain to him how passion, madness, murder, and sex-switching are linked:

Oh! Disgust you! I am sure that the opposite would be true. Here is my conclusion. If I were a girl, I could not help loving you, and I know it. But because I am a boy, it is my duty not to accommodate your desires in the least, for your passion, which at this moment is only natural, would then instantly become monstrous. Your ardent nature would become the enemy

of your reason, and even your reason would become so easily accommodating that it would enter into complicity with your misguided intentions
and join forces with your nature. This revelation that you ask of me—so
likely to inflame you, yet that you seem to welcome rather than to fear—
would make you lose control of yourself. Seeking what they could not
find, your eyes and hands would want to avenge themselves on what they
did find, and you and I would commit all that is most abominable between men. With such an enlightened mind, how can you flatter yourself
by imagining that you would stop loving me if you discovered that I was
a man? Do you believe that my charms, as you call them (and consider
so enamoring), would disappear? You must realize that they might well
increase in force, and that your passion, brutal by this point, would try
all of the means invented by your enamored mind to calm itself. You
would end by persuading yourself that you could transform me into a
woman; or thinking yourself capable of becoming a woman yourself, you
would want me to treat you as such. Seduced by your passion, your reason
would create countless sophisms. You would say that your love for me, as
a man, is more reasonable than it would be if I were a girl, for you would
seek to locate its source in the purest kind of friendship; and you would
not fail to offer me examples of such extravagances. Seduced yourself by
the false brilliance of your false reasons, you would become a torrent that
no dam could hold back, and I would run out of words to combat your
false reasons and exhaust my strength in fighting off your violent fury. You
would end up threatening to kill me if I forbade you from penetrating an
inviolable temple whose door was wisely designed by nature to open only
as an exit.   (2: 18–19)

Bellino's answer can be read as a defense against the unleashing
of a homosexuality that he considers monstrous. It is as if he were
saying: even if you proved that I am a boy, you would nonetheless
proceed to the act. He suspects, in fact, that it is the ambiguity of
his identity that excites Casanova: "Seeking what they could not
find, your eyes and hands would want to avenge themselves on
what they did find" (2: 18). Bellino's fears are not unfounded, for
although Casanova had seen him to be "truly a man" (2: 14), Casanova had made this confession a bit earlier: "I told him that because
these eyes were a woman's and not a man's, I needed to convince
myself through touch that what I had seen while he was fending
me off was not a monstrous clitoris" (2: 16). This is obviously a
central issue for Casanova, what he would like ultimately to see and
touch: a woman with a monstrous clitoris upon which he could not

help avenging himself, for it is this alliance that he finds both fascinating and unbearable.

There is, however, something else that is undoubtedly the only method at Casanova's disposal for resolving this dilemma, a factor that first emerged in his dialogues with Nanette and Marton—namely, to reverse genders by passing from one to the other: "You would end by persuading yourself that you could transform me into a woman; or thinking yourself capable of becoming a woman yourself, you would want me to treat you as such" (2: 19). Evoking homosexuality only serves to transform the man into a woman, because the woman has become a man. What had been a game with three women recognized as such (Nanette, Marton, and Angela) takes on tragic proportions in the dual relationship with a man suspected of being a woman.

It is said that love is blind; to be precise, we should say that love is founded upon the possibility of not knowing. To be ignorant of the other's gender and forget one's own, to be able to make the other a different or an identical gender and do the same for oneself—this is the height of passionate love. But the uncertainty that sends one into raptures carries with it a long trail of threats, fury, and death: "You would become a torrent that no dam could hold back. . . . You would end up threatening to kill me" (2: 19). For the person who is the object of one's passions is not entitled to be what he is, or, for that matter, to let himself become something other than what he is. A lover can no more bear to see the other submit and bend to the changing winds of love than he can tolerate any hint that his beloved might resist the pressure to be indeterminate. This is how love can be fatal, ending in a mixture of frenzy and murder. In love, one cannot stand that the other not remain fixed in his alterity, well distinguished, separated, different—or that he not be indefinitely malleable to one's changing whims, ready at a moment's notice to assume the mask of the desired figure, a figure whose diverse possibilities are represented by the opposition of the two sexes.

Casanova had let it be known that he was on the brink of madness: "Allow me to assume that, knowing that you looked exactly like a girl, you devised the cruel scheme of making me fall in love with you, only to drive me mad by withholding from me a firm conviction, which alone could restore my reason" (2: 16). One of the causes of madness resides precisely in the impossibility of determining gender—that is, the inability to maintain sexual difference. What disappears in such a case is one of the essential pillars offered by culture for distinguishing individuals. When sexual difference is erased, the principle of individuation loses its bearings, paving the way to indeterminacy and the abolition of all other differences. But to reach the limit of this difference—which is one of the Promethean enterprises that underlies Casanova's life—would also mean attaining an unlimited sort of power, a power that could transform passionate love life into a celebration with no future, by doing away with all temporal imperatives.

Bellino senses that he is caught in this infernal whirlwind, in which he no longer knows who or what he is. He resists with all of his might and all of his intellectual subtlety, and reveals in the process what Casanova had been unable to admit to himself without overstepping the boundary of mental imbalance. But then there occurs a dramatic turn of events:

> After requesting that our trunks be untied and carried into a suitable room, I ordered supper. Seeing that there was only one bed in the room, I asked Bellino in a very calm voice whether he wished to have a fire kindled in another room. He surprised me by answering gently that he would not mind in the least sleeping in my bed.
>
> The reader can easily imagine my astonishment upon hearing this answer, which I could never have expected, and which I so greatly needed to dispel the dark mood that was tormenting my mind. (2: 20)

As readers, we are truly astonished by this reversal. Why, after putting up such a splendid defense, does Bellino give up so abruptly and, without saying a word, show that he is a woman after all? Why indeed, if not because of his singular life story, which only Casanova's uniquely intense passion was able to unravel. Bellino now reveals that he (or she) is named Thérèse, the daughter of an employee of the Institute of Bologna, where she had met Salimbani, a famous castrato musician. Salimbani takes Thérèse under his protection and teaches her to play the harpsichord and sing. This is what happens:

> Salimbani was keeping a boy my age in the home of a music teacher in Rimini; the boy had been mutilated on the order of his dying father in order to preserve his voice and provide a source of income for his large family, whom he could support by appearing on stage. This boy, whose name was

Bellino, was the son of the good woman whom you just met in Ancona, and whom everyone believes to be my mother. (2: 23)

A year later, Thérèse's father dies, and she is left an orphan. Salimbani brings her to Rimini so that she can become the student of Bellino's music teacher. But then, the day before their arrival, Bellino (the real brother of Marine and Cécile) dies. Salimbani has the rather farfetched idea of "taking Thérèse back to Bologna under the name of the same Bellino who had just died" and having her stay with the deceased boy's mother, "who, in her poverty, would find it profitable to keep the secret." Salimbani explains to Thérèse the details of how she will have to conduct herself if she is to take the place of a castrato:

All that you must do is to make the people of Bologna believe that you are Bellino, which should be easy for you, since no one knows you. Only Bellino's mother will know the truth. Her children will not question that you are their brother, for they were very young when I sent him to Rimini. If you love me, you must renounce your sex and forget the very memory of it. As of this moment you must take the name Bellino and leave with me immediately for Bologna. In two hours you will see yourself dressed as a boy: your sole concern will be to prevent anyone from recognizing that you are a girl. You will sleep alone; you will be careful while dressing; and when, in a year or two, your bosom develops, have no worry, for having an excessively large chest is the ordinary defect of all of us. Aside from all this, before leaving I will give you a little apparatus and teach you how to apply it so adroitly to the spot that shows sexual differences that people will be fooled easily if it should happen that you must undergo an examination. (2: 24–25)

How on earth did Casanova manage to find such a rare bird, one who fits so perfectly all he was looking for? When one reads his *Memoirs*, one occasionally wonders whether this is not all a pure novel, the fiction that conforms most closely to the author's phantasms and mode of psychic functioning. After all, it has already been frequently suggested that, in order for Casanova's love life to be played out, he needs to be ignorant, to fool himself about gender and identity. What had been only faintly perceptible before becomes clearly visible in the adventure with Bellino. For Bellino is true neither to her gender nor to her identity. Her mother and sisters are not her own, and she—Thérèse as Bellino—is a man who has forgotten even the memory of his real gender. Because men had to disguise themselves as women in order to play a feminine role on stage, Bellino had to pass for a man in the theater of life.

If we were to suppose that this paradigmatic story were true, what would have occurred between Thérèse and Casanova? For Casanova, it is a great stroke of luck to meet a woman who is a man under an assumed name—a name with which she has come to identify. The greater the trickery involved, the more likely Casanova will fall madly in love; so he was not about to miss such an opportunity. As for Thérèse, she confesses that "I had resolved to give myself to you as soon as you had taken me away from Ancona, from the very moment that I bid Cécile to go ask if you wished to escort me to Rimini" (2: 28). Translated into our terms, that means: I was resolved to give myself to you once you had taken the risk of bringing me along with you without knowing who I was. But why is there this long waiting period, seemingly so sincere? Without the battle and debate between the two of them, neither would have realized the reason for their love. Bellino had to expose the fact that Casanova's passion was founded in the indeterminacy of gender and identity, before Thérèse could appear as loved precisely because she is wounded. She had been wounded by being forced to live under a false identity and a false gender. To be healed, she had to be desired as wounded—that is, as a man, which she is not on two counts: first, because she is a woman; and second, because she bears the name of another man. She had to seduce Casanova by deceiving him about her gender and her identity in order to be rid of this very deception. For her, nothing would have happened, and she would not have given herself to Casanova, if he had wanted to possess her as he would any woman; he had to travel the path that 'she herself had taken.

In the midst of their long explanations, Thérèse tells him of the apparatus that "makes the feminine disappear" (2: 25) and then shows it to him:

She got out of bed, poured water into a goblet, opened her trunk, and pulled out her apparatus and her glues, put them on, and adjusted the mask. I saw something incredible. A charming girl, who appeared to be just that in every feature, seemed even more interesting to me with this extraordinary apparatus, because this white pendant posed no obstacle to her feminine reservoir. I told her that she had been wise not to allow me to touch her, for she would have made me drunk with passion, and turned me into what I was not, unless she had first calmed me by revealing the truth. I wanted to convince her that I was not lying, and our debate was comical. (2: 28)

We have heard Casanova's comment quite clearly: "A charming girl . . . seemed even more interesting to me with this extraordinary apparatus." It is, therefore, true that he has little interest in men, but great interest in a woman who takes on a masculine appearance. His mind starts scheming, and he wants Thérèse to be his for life by "fixing this union with the seal of marriage" (2: 29). He informs her of his decision: "The day after tomorrow, and no later, I will marry you in Bologna, for I want you to belong to me by every bond imaginable" (2: 31). Yet he has hardly declared his intentions when a minor hitch—happenstance, as always—arises that will prevent him from carrying out his plans.

In Pesaro, along the route to Rimini, they are stopped by Spanish soldiers, who ask to see their passports. Thérèse complies, but Casanova cannot find his, although he had filed it with some letters of recommendation that he was carrying with him. Thérèse continues her journey, but Casanova will have to remain in Pesaro to wait for a new passport. In truth, he does not remain there. A few days after his arrival, he comes upon a horse whose rider, an officer, has just dismounted. Without any plan in mind, he mounts the horse; and the horse takes off like a shot, passes the last Spanish outpost, and does not calm down until he is among Austrian soldiers. Casanova joins Thérèse in Rimini, but, since he still has no passport, he cannot stay. He tells himself that he is still just as infatuated with her, but he also knows that he has freed himself of a long-lasting tie. A lost passport prevents him from crossing borders; but, by getting lost at the right moment, it also keeps him from crossing the most fearsome border of all—marriage. One may wonder whether everything that had made Thérèse so seductive—the fact that the reality she presented corresponded so well to Casanova's most deeply ingrained phantasms—did not fade away as soon as all doubt was dispelled, and she could no longer serve as a support for those phantasms.

A Uniform on a Whim

CASANOVA has already demonstrated more than once that, to succeed in love, he must be able to confuse personal identity and gender. We should specify, however, that although he does not want to recognize gender differences and identity distinctions, he is fully aware of them. In other words, as long as it is Casanova who creates uncertainty, he can control what he sees or does not see—that is, he can manipulate his mask like a set of blinders. In such a situation, the resulting confusion allows him to avoid the anguish of having to confront a particular person or gender, a well-defined other. He is aroused when, in the throes of passion, he can take the male or female he has before him for someone else. This is what occurred with Nanette and Marton. When he meets Bellino, the situation is reversed: he doubts, he does not know, and this triggers within him a veritable fury to know, see, and touch. In this case, the uncertainty surrounding sexual and identity distinctions is imposed upon him by his partner, and Casanova reacts by ripping off the disguise worn by Bellino-Thérèse to oblige her to resolve it. To ward off impending madness, Casanova feels the imperious need to return to reality and reject all deception. Such an unmasking calms his fury, but of course his passion is snuffed out in the process.

The adventure with Bellino-Thérèse comprises the first two chapters of the second volume of the *Memoirs*. It is no surprise that chapter 3, in which Thérèse leaves for Naples by herself (2: 46–48), brings us back to Venice for a new (and final) tryst with Nanette and Marton (2: 51). The circle of knowledge and anti-knowledge is now complete. These two terms had to meet in a literary sense, because the inversion of sexual roles and imagined identities that marked his first sexual experience is complemented by the episode that reestablishes Thérèse in her true gender and identity.

This completion of Casanova's first love persona is underscored in many ways in this third chapter. Up to this point, the story of his life had developed against the backdrop of an ecclesiastic career. Casanova brings this to an end by dressing up as a military man, having a tailor fit him out in an "impromptu uniform, sure that I would not be forced to account for my business to anyone" (2: 42). In this instance, the libertine is above all a libertarian who will not submit to any authority. "Having just left the ranks of two armies, in which I had seen no respect accorded to any garb but military uniforms, I too wanted to become respectable. I also thought it would be great fun to return to my native city in the trappings of honor, a city where I had been considerably mistreated while wearing church garb" (2: 42). There is no basis for his military title other than his clothing, yet he is thrilled to attract curious gazes and hear people whispering about him. A Monsignor Cornaro, whom Casanova had met in Venice and Rome, recognizes him. Far from unmasking the young abbé, this prelate gives him the gazette article that will allow him to pass for someone else and give a doubly appropriated credibility to his appearance. As we recall, Casanova, when arrested in Pesaro for lack of a passport, mounted a horse that took off like lightning and brought him to an Austrian military camp. From there, he managed to return to Venice. These were the facts of his most recent adventure. But what is reported in the article of the Pesaro gazette is this: "M. de Casanova, an officer of the queen's regiment, has deserted, after killing his captain in a duel. No one knows the circumstances of this duel; all that is known is that the aforementioned officer set out en route for Rimini on the horse of his captain, who was left dead" (2: 44–45). Casanova comments:

Chuckling to myself about all of these false rumors, and about the circumstances that combined to lend them an air of credibility, I became from this point on a resolved skeptic on the subject of so-called historical truths. I took real pleasure in assuming a reserved air and thus feeding Abbé Cornaro's belief that I was the same Casanova as the one described by the Pesaro gazette. I was sure that he would write as much to the authorities in Venice, and the rumor would do me honor there, at least until the truth was finally discovered, and my resolve would then be justified. For this reason I decided to go to Venice as soon as I received a letter from Thérèse. I thought of asking her to come to Venice, since I could wait for her there much more comfortably than in Bologna; and nothing would have prevented me from marrying her in my native city. In the meantime, this fable amused me. Every day I expected to see the truth revealed in the gazette. The officer Casanova must have laughed to hear that, according to the Pesaro gazette reporter, he had left on a horse, just as I laughed about the whim that had inspired me to dress as an officer in Bologna and thus provide substance for the whole tale. (2: 45–46)

Finding himself—by chance, of course—the subject of a fable, and labeled, on the basis of what he did, the culprit of something he did not do, yet for which he gets the glory, our "novice impostor" (2: 44) regains his confidence and proceeds to buy a real officer's title in order to give weight to the title he had usurped. Thanks to a gazette that concocted a tall tale, his assumed appearance becomes the authentic starting point for a new career. As with Bellino-Thérèse, what Casanova constructs in his imagination finds an unexpected mirror image in reality.

This third chapter of volume 2—in which truth and falsehood are so intertwined that Casanova becomes more and more skeptical "on the subject of so-called historical truths"—is an excellent introduction to chapters 4, 5, and 6, which relate Casanova's journey to Constantinople and Corfu. Casanova specialists agree that these chapters are in fact a condensed account of his two stays in these cities, one in 1741, the other in 1745. He may even have spiced up his story with anecdotes that he probably heard but did not experience firsthand. The fact that these pages are especially perplexing for historians gives reasonable cause to assume that their composition is calculated. What then is the message he wants to impart at a juncture that marks the end of the first stage of his life—that is, his first attempt at combining imagination with reality? With his adolescence now behind him, Casanova must take another step forward and confront obstacles more formidable than those he has avoided up to this point. That is, he must confront

enemies that he had sought to minimize, for they now rise up before him and must be overcome if he is to establish the reign of
universal liberty and laughter; in a word, he must confront religion
and women, all women who leave no doubt about their gender. In
Constantinople, he will use his conversations with Muslims to undermine both their religion and his own, all the while maintaining
a solemn tone. In Corfu, a woman will keep him at a tormenting
distance. In Constantinople, he will strip the heavens of any authority over him. In Corfu, he will be turned away from the "para-
dise" (2: 167) of woman.

Now a military man, Casanova starts by settling his accounts
with religion, which he feels has "mistreated" him (2: 42). This is
undoubtedly one of the reasons that he erased from his *Memoirs* all
mention of his journey to Constantinople when he was sixteen
years old. Because he was destined at the time for a career in the
Church, Casanova would have been less apt to lend a sympathetic
ear to his Muslim friends' critiques of Christianity. In the discussions that he relates here, he nevertheless takes care to affirm that
he is a Christian, faithful to the religion of his father (2: 78), and he
does not hesitate to describe the less savory aspects of his hosts'
practices.

The tone is set at the beginning of chapter 4 by the tale of an
adventure that occurs on the boat bringing Casanova to Constantinople. (The chapter actually begins with a different anecdote,
whose significance will become clear at the end of my Chapter 6.)
A tempest has arisen, and a priest is performing exorcisms to chase
away the devils; as a result, the sailors on the boat neglect "the
maneuvers necessary to keep the vessel away from the rocks visible
left and right" (2: 61). Casanova urges them to work "by telling
them that there were no devils, and that the priest, who claimed
there were, was raving mad." But the priest avenges himself by
calling Casanova an atheist and explaining that the tempest had
been brought on by an evil parchment in the possession of this
officer. Casanova barely avoids getting himself killed, his parchment is seized and burned, and the tempest subsides. This is the
singular commentary offered by our crusader against superstition:
"The so-called magical property of this parchment was to make all
women fall in love with the person carrying it. I hope that the

reader will be good enough to believe that I had no faith in any sort of love potions, and that I had only bought the parchment for a halfpenny to have a good laugh" (2: 62).

When we remember the role played by magic throughout Casanova's life, we might suspect that his laughter is not entirely sincere, and that the religions he hopes to undermine through ridicule have left traces (seen here in their elementary forms) that he will never succeed in erasing.

In Constantinople, he meets three people. The first is a renegade, the count of Bonneval, who has come to Turkey to avoid the galleys and to become a pasha of Carmania. He represents the tranquil unbeliever who "was Turkish just as he had been Christian, and who knew the Koran no better than he knew the Bible" (2: 68). A military man more than a skeptic, the count had left Europe because he could no longer practice his profession there; and he enjoys the tolerance of Islam, which does not require him to believe and allows him to have a library filled not with books, but with good wine, a French butler, and a "cook [who was] also an honest renegade" (2: 69). In a word, he is the person who will introduce Casanova to his Turkish friends, a guide who has learned how to reduce religions to their minimal degree of impact.

The second person contrasts with the first as well as with the third. He is a "rich and wise philosopher, of widely recognized integrity, whose moral purity equaled his attachment to his religion" (2: 70). Casanova has long conversations with him that range from the pleasures of the pipe (focusing particularly on the sight of smoke leaving one's mouth) to the immateriality of God and his non-composition, contrasted to the Christian notion of God as a trinity. But the goal of the Venetian officer is to dismiss both religions by comparing them to each other, so as to free himself of any ties to either:

As I was returning to my quarters, I reflected that it was quite possible that everything Josouff had told me about the essence of God was true, for certainly *the being of beings* could not be anything in essence but the most simple of beings; but I could not possibly let myself be persuaded, as a consequence of an error in the Christian religion, to embrace the Turkish religion, which might well have a very accurate idea of *God*, but which made me laugh, inasmuch as its doctrine derived from one of the most extravagant impostors of all time. (2: 78)

After some discussions on marriage, chastity, and masturbation (all occasions for Casanova to slip in a few subversive thoughts), Josouff offers him his daughter in marriage, on the condition that he become a Muslim. Casanova thinks this would truly be too high a price to pay for a beauty whom he has not even been able to see face-to-face; but he is nevertheless impressed by this paternal figure, whose traits he will later recognize on "the handsome face of M. de Bragadin, a Venetian senator" (2: 189). As we shall soon see, Bragadin does not ask such a price for his paternity—a paternity for which Casanova feels a need, provided that he can adapt it to his tastes.

Ismail is the third person. This is a man of pleasures. One day, he invites Casanova "to take a stroll in a little garden, where in a secluded nook he had an inspiration that I did not find to my liking; I told him, laughing, that I did not go in for such things" (2: 80). Ismail will have his way, however, after a few detours. While entertaining one evening, he gives the Venetian the opportunity (rare in Constantinople) to dance a furlana with a comely compatriot. On another occasion, he takes Casanova on a fishing excursion that ends in a study from which one can look into another room without being seen.

We saw, almost directly before our eyes, three girls who were stark naked, at times swimming, at times getting out of the water to rest on marble perches where, standing or sitting, they dried themselves off and exposed themselves in every imaginable position. This charming spectacle could not fail to excite me immediately, and Ismail, swooning with joy, convinced me that I should not restrain myself; he encouraged me instead to give myself over to the effects that this voluptuous sight must certainly have aroused in my soul, by offering himself as an example. I found myself forced, like him, to make do with the object I had next to me in order to quench the fire that had been sparked by the three sirens. (2: 92–93)

This is one of the few homosexual adventures recounted in the *Memoirs*; Ismail has thus gotten what he wanted. But for the story that is under way at this moment, the background to this episode is what is most important. For Casanova, Turkey will come to represent the place where feminine beauty remains beyond his reach.

In the pages that follow, he has a conversation alone with Josouff's wife, who does everything to arouse him, but sharply calls him back to order when he dares to lift the veil hiding her face.

All of these unattainable women seem to serve here as an introduction to the love story that will become Casanova's sole preoccupation during his stay in Corfu. As in Venice with Angela or in Rome with Marquise G., he meets up with yet another inaccessible woman. He had been named adjutant (that is, warrant officer) to assist one M.D.R., commanding officer of a section of the Venetian flotilla; in keeping with the customs of the day, M.D.R. is also the protector of a lady referred to as Mme F., identified as Foscarini. Under orders to M.D.R., Casanova belongs to his household and hence often finds himself in the company of this lady. Unfortunately for him, she is one of those women for whom the supreme danger is to satisfy their desires, and for whom survival is possible only by maintaining a state of unfulfilled desire. This is a characteristic that lends itself well to the makings of a long story.

At first, Mme F. grants Casanova neither the slightest word nor look. And she only speaks to him later in order to humiliate him. He starts to detest her. As he writes, "This young woman was the source of my unhappiness, and I was angry with myself, for if I had not felt such hate for her, I would never have given her the least thought" (2: 103). But why does he feel such hate that he cannot turn away from her? Why does he accept a position that turns him into a pawn: "Because she was so young and felt the urge to amuse herself, she had chosen me as an object of diversion just as she would have chosen a puppet" (2: 104)?

When she asks him for money to pay off one of her husband's gambling debts, Casanova thinks for a brief moment that everything is going to change. She remains, however, as haughty as ever. When the adjutant assures her that no man could refuse her such a small service, she replies: "What you tell me is very flattering, but I hope that I shall never again find myself in the awful situation of having to ask for your services." Casanova concludes: "I had figured it all out. I saw that she guarded her glory jealously, and I adored her" (2: 106). He is thus caught more inextricably in the trap, and his only resource is to remain calm, for he has no means of advancing on his own:

Everything that I did and said when Mme F. was present was aimed solely at pleasing her; but because I never looked at her when it was not called for, I never gave her a hint that I sought only to please her. I wanted to break her down and arouse her curiosity, make her suspect the truth, guess my secret. In the meantime I enjoyed seeing that my money and good conduct won me a consideration that I could not have hoped to attain from my employment or my age, nor from any talent to be expected in the profession that I had undertaken. (2: 107)

Mme F. nonetheless continues to play the tease, acting warm and cold by turns. She makes him recount the story of his adventures in Constantinople, insisting particularly that he give details about the "night spent with Ismail spying on his bathing mistresses" (2: 131). Yet nothing comes of it, for she uses the story to ridicule him by asking him to tell the same story in public, sparing no details. When Casanova declines, seconded by M.D.R., she retorts, "If it would be wrong for him to tell such a story to the whole group, then he also was wrong to tell it to me" (2: 135). Despite this treacherous game, in which Mme F. uses and abuses her authority over the defenseless adjutant, Casanova is as persistent as ever: "I hid my vexation, and we left fifteen minutes later. I was learning to know her to the core; I could foresee the cruel tests to which she would put me; but love promised me victory and commanded me to hope" (2: 135).

The same game continues until one day when, because her chambermaid is absent, the lady asks Casanova to suck her finger, which she had pricked, "to draw out the blood." Casanova comments:

If my reader has ever been in love, he can imagine how I performed this task; for what, after all, is a kiss? It is nothing but the true effect of a desire to draw from one's beloved. After thanking me, she told me to spit out what I had sucked into my hankerchief.

"I swallowed it, madame, and Lord knows with what pleasure."

"Swallowed my blood with pleasure? Do you come from a race of cannibals?" (2: 137)

Indeed, is there not something cannibalistic in this love affair? Casanova will later eat her hair, and they will speak of feeding their tender sentiments. Their game continues: the more he pursues her, the more she fends him off. On one occasion, she wants to repay

71

him the money she had borrowed, but he has arranged to have the sum erased from the note on which the debt had been registered. Mme F. reacts in her usual fashion: "In the days that followed, she seized every occasion possible to quibble with me. . . . When I was recounting some amusing story, she would pretend not to understand the joke. . . . Her behavior made me visibly moody, and she would pretend not to notice. . . . When I was alone, I often cried" (2: 142–43).

Although the same pattern of alternating seductions and rebuffs continues, Mme F. nevertheless arranges, after prolonged hesitation, for the adjutant to come stay in her home and lodges him, moreover, in a room connected to her own. This serves as an opportunity for the author of the *Memoirs* to write us a couplet to love, calling it madness and illness. He is indeed correct in this case, for the two adjoining rooms meet at an angle, allowing Casanova and Mme F. to see each other all the time. Hence Casanova lives in this woman's constant presence and directly under her gaze, while she manages to create an infinite distance in their proximity: "Three weeks went by, but my new lodgings brought no relief to my ardor. All that I told myself, in order not to lose hope, was that her love was not yet strong enough to overcome her pride. . . . What annoyed me most were the distinctions she accorded me in public, whereas, in private, she was stingy; I wished that it could be the contrary" (2: 142–43). The torture attains new heights of refinement:

I could have watched her getting out of bed, and relish her in my enamored imagination; and she could have granted me this balm for my ardor without compromising herself in the least, for she need not have bothered to guess whether I was watching. But she did not do this. It seemed that she only opened her windows to torment me. I could see her in her bed. Her chambermaid would come to dress her and would stand in front of her so that I could no longer see her. If, after leaving her bed, she did go to the window to see how the weather was, she would not glance at the windows of my room. I was sure she knew I was watching her; but she did not want to grant me the small pleasure of making some gesture that might make me conjecture that she was thinking of me.   (2: 151)

One day, he discreetly gathers "the split ends of her long hair" (2: 152), which she had just had cut. She catches him in the act and forces him to give them back, which literally makes him ill; she revives him by returning his booty. He makes a bracelet and a braid out of some of this hair and grinds the rest of it into a powder that he has mixed into candies. This allows him to eat her. From this point on, he no longer hides his passion, but professes it openly to her; she too admits that she loves him, but nonetheless demands that he control himself.

A few days later, she gives him a kiss, and then more kisses; and when Casanova asks her if that is as far as they will go, she answers, "My dear friend, we shall never go any further. Love is a child that we must appease with trifles, for a true feast would only kill it" (2: 160). While out for a stroll, she injures her leg, shows him the wound, and allows him to touch her. Then she lets him see all of her. But even then, "she positioned herself so that it was impossible for me to penetrate the sanctuary; and she always took care to prohibit my hands from making any movement that could expose her eyes to a sight that would have broken down all her defenses" (2: 164). They spend a night together, but for her, the act of abandoning herself is always tied to the ultimate refusal:

Ah! My beloved friend! There is a furnace there. How can your finger linger there without being burned by the fire that devours me? Ah! My friend! Stop. Hold me as tight as you can. Approach the tomb, but take care not to bury yourself there. . . . I loved you fifteen minutes ago, and now I love you even more: I would love you less if you had exhausted all of my joy by fulfilling all of my desires. (2: 166–67)

Images of the tomb and of death recur over and over again in these pages. Mme F. explains quite clearly that, for her, there is no desire without hope, no desire that must not be deferred. She considers her genitals analogous to a tomb because, for her, satisfaction, final satisfaction, would be nothing less than the death of desire—in other words, death pure and simple. She could not survive being satiated. For her, desire cannot be fulfilled in reality, because she would compare it with what she had anticipated. As she says, "At the convent, my imagination was my greatest resource" (2: 168). It is for this reason that she and Casanova are bound to break up; and their rupture occurs just as they are about to carry their passions all the way:

She sits down at the foot of the bed and looks at me; I fall into her arms burning with love; she gives herself to me and allows me to penetrate the sanctuary, and my soul at last swims in happiness; but she keeps me there only an instant. She does not allow me to enjoy for a full second the indescribable pleasure of knowing that I am master of a treasure; she pulls back suddenly, pushes me away and gets up, then throws herself, with a distraught look, upon an armchair. Immobile, astonished, and trembling, I look at her, trying to understand what could have caused this unnatural movement; and I hear her say to me, while gazing at me with piercing, loving eyes,

"My dear friend, we were about to lose ourselves."

"What, lose? You have killed me. Alas! I can feel that I am dying. You may never see me again." (2: 170)

Disconcerted, Casanova—sure that he is "positively dying"—goes out to the street where he meets a prostitute named Melulla, and with her he commits outrages against his beloved. Mme F., who had noticed her friend's absence, forces him to confess everything the next day, and this ends what had been between them. Sometime later, Casanova returns to Venice, where he gives up his military uniform.

This story had to be recounted in its entirety because it is typical of one aspect of Casanova's love life. To succeed in love, he employs two or three preestablished schemes, and each time he deviates from them (as he will try to do again), he fails. Some readers will probably say that social circumstances were not favorable to him. The wife of a Venetian nobleman was obliged to resist any advances from a lowly adjutant officer. That is certainly true, but it does not address the real problem. Casanova is fascinated by Mme F., finds her desirable, and persists in his pursuit of her precisely because she is a very particular kind of woman: she represents all the women who have made him suffer, who have both inspired great passions and set murderous traps for him. Mme F. recalls Bettine—neither a madwoman nor a witch—but she also prefigures Miss Charpillon of London, who will mark the end of Casanova's life as a young fledgling libertine. A reader who is wise to the beginning of the *Memoirs* would have known from the start that this love affair was doomed to fail simply because it lacked the necessary preparations. If Casanova has neither a pair of sisters nor any doubt about gender, he cannot gain access to the woman in question. Any woman who shows no ambiguity about her gender is inaccessible—this is the rule, and perhaps the warning, with which Casanova leaves us here.

We could say that Casanova's failure with Mme F. stems from the character of this woman, for whom having no desire (even for a second) is tantamount to losing everything—that is, tantamount to death—because, in such an instance, she is no longer sure she can arouse a man's desire and be the object of that desire. And if she can no longer attract a man's hopeful gaze, then there is no more point to her existence, for she knows that she would then lose herself in the other and be lost for him. As she herself says so well, "This abstinence will make our love immortal" (2: 167), because it maintains between them the minimal distance necessary to keep them both from disappearing.

Immortality is made to exclude time. The act of fulfilling desire, even when achieved simultaneously, would force lovers to think of real successions, relative bonds, moments of banality. In Casanova's view, love must remain in a smoldering state of extreme tension, of crisis, of infinite power; what he asks of these women is to keep him at the height of anticipation—and hence at the height of eternity, or at least of suspended time. In spite of the ordeals he knew he would have to endure, he is unable to turn away from Mme F. (as he had been with Bettine and will later be with Miss Charpillon) because this woman tells him: with me, you will never cease to desire, desire will always sustain you, and you will be saved from time by promises of always, endlessly, waiting. And if he falls into this pattern again and again, it is probably because he tells himself that, this time, it will work.

There is yet another reason for Casanova's failure, whose significance will become apparent later. He not only gives up religious garb, but seeks to rid himself of all religion by combining a critique of Islam and Christianity; and in the process, he meets a feminine prototype utterly lacking the symbolic foundation, the justification and support, that are provided by a cultural community. Moreover, because he does not make use of his customary veil of ignorance concerning gender and identity, the failure of his romantic undertaking proves fatal. Casanova cannot attain a woman unless he is protected by a set of cultural values or by a set of blinders; otherwise, he sinks into a state of sordidness in which women are mere trash.

That is why this military episode begins in chapter 3 with the comical description of an earlier case of venereal disease (which had been a great boon for a "surgeon"; 2: 59), and ends with another case of V.D. passed on by the prostitute Melulla at the moment of Casanova's breakup with Mme F. It is as if Casanova wanted to suggest that neither his comprehensive questioning of religion nor his quest for the impossible woman succeeded in warding off the shadow of a horror always ready to reemerge. He will have to invent other detours if he is to recover his liberty and laughter.

I have not yet mentioned a particular episode related in these chapters, the one that concerns his brief stay in Caproso. The author of the *Memoirs* has already accustomed us to the art of counterpoint. To dramatize this tale—in which women seem irreparably distant, and the young officer appears to be an ineffective flatterer—Casanova places an adventure at the very center of these chapters (2: 108–28) that presents him as the hero in unveiling an impostor, after which he is forced to take flight. He settles on an island and surrounds himself with a troop of men to defend him and a group of girls to attend to his pleasures. The pages of these chapters that dwell on Casanova's failures are thus set into relief by his dazzling triumphs as an apprentice war chief and make-believe sultan.

By Magic

Now all hell breaks loose. Upon his return to Venice, Casanova finds a place (through the intervention of Abbé Grimani) as a violinist in the orchestra of the San Samuele Theater. But he spends his nights with a band of hoodlums, "inventing and executing every audacity we could imagine" (2: 183)—like untying gondolas from their docks; waking up midwives, doctors, and priests under the pretext of an emergency; bothering prostitutes' clients; and organizing gang rapes; not to mention stirring up early-morning ruckuses and hurling insults. In a word, at the age of twenty, Casanova becomes "an out-and-out good-for-nothing" (2: 182).

Fortune, however, is watching over him. One night, while returning home after having performed as violinist at a wedding ball, he picks up a letter that had fallen from the pocket of a "senator garbed in red" (2: 189). Casanova hands the senator his letter and is invited to board his gondola. A few minutes later, the senator has an attack. After bleeding the patient, Casanova takes him home to his palace and calls for a doctor, who prescribes "an ointment of mercury on the chest" (2: 191). M. de Bragadin (that is the senator's name) is on the point of suffocating during the night, so Casanova rips off the mercury plaster and saves the noble Venetian. The violinist is transformed into a doctor who pontificates like a scholar, citing authors he has never read. M. de Bragadin, who "is interested in the abstract sciences" (2: 193), is convinced that this young man "possesses some supernatural power":

> He begged me to tell him the truth. It was at that moment that, not wanting to offend his vanity by insisting that he was mistaken, I chose the odd solution of telling him and two of his friends who were also there a wild, utterly false story about a numerical calculation I claimed to know, which would answer a question—written down and changed into numbers—with a response (also in numbers) telling me everything that I wanted to know, and that no one could have told me otherwise. M. de Bragadin said that this was Solomon's clavicula,* commonly known as the cabala. (2: 193)

Casanova asserts that, according to the monk who revealed it to him, he would be struck down dead within three days if he passed on his secret. Bragadin and the two friends living with him ask no more and take full advantage of the gifts of their guest, who welcomes any opportunity to reinforce their gullibility. The cabala is never wrong, because its interpreter is wise enough to give two answers, "one of which would become apparent only after the event, because he alone knew it" (2: 195).

Thus begins Casanova's career as a charlatan and con man. He can find no better justification for his new endeavor than the impossibility of forcing these venerable gentlemen to abandon their belief in all the various forms of occultism, and the necessity of meeting his ever-pressing expenses incurred by a life of pleasure. We should probably not take Bragadin and his friends to be more naïve than they are. As Félicien Marceau observes, "I wonder whether, however impressed they may be by Casanova's knowledge on this subject, these three gentlemen—who must not have too many distractions—might not in fact be grateful to him for bringing them his loquaciousness, his good humor, the tales of his escapades, in short, his youth."†

The fact remains that Bragadin, recovered from his illness after a few weeks, makes this speech to Casanova:

> Whoever you are, I owe you my life. Your protectors, who wanted to make you a priest, a doctor of theology, a lawyer, a soldier, and then a violin

---

*This is a reference to the *Clavicula Salomonis*, a medieval book of magic.
† *Une Insolente Liberté: les aventures de Casanova* (Gallimard, 1983), p. 101.

player, were nothing but a bunch of fools who did not know you. God ordered your guardian angel to lead you into my hands. I understood you; if you wish to be my son, you need only recognize me as your father, and from that point on I shall treat you as a son in my house until I die. Your apartment is ready, so have your belongings brought there; you shall have a servant, and a paid gondola, a welcome at our table, and ten sequins a month. (2: 198)

This is a turning point in Casanova's life. He will remain attached to this man, calling him father henceforth in the story, and undoubtedly considering him to be that. He will maintain his ties to Bragadin until the man's death in 1767—yet he never hesitates to solicit Bragadin's aid when his money runs out.

This is, however, a singular situation, for the roles of father and son are reversed. At the age of twenty-one, when one would normally have taken a certain distance from one's father, Casanova (who scarcely knew his own father) meets a man who offers to play this role for him. Bragadin is hardly a father whom he would like to see dead, according to the well-known adage; to the contrary, Casanova has saved this man's life. Moreover, this father, who should stand for some form of rigor, unwittingly offers Casanova an opportunity to become an impostor. It is in relation to Bragadin that Casanova practices his talents as con man for the first time in his life. These scenes contain a burlesque dimension that does not escape the notice of our memoirist. It is, however, a burlesque charged with meaning—in fact, it reveals a structural trait of Casanova's personality. Although he appears to be entirely submissive and avoids all the traits typical of a rebellious son, Casanova nonetheless subverts the father-son bond from within. His father is paternal by becoming his son's dupe, by adhering to a ridiculous belief encouraged by this son.

This episode in Casanova's life is decisive, not only because magic makes its appearance in the form of the cabala, but also because it presents itself as exactly what it is: an act staged in order to evade the law of the father (that is, of any authority) by mimicking that law through the purported communication with higher powers, and, more significantly, by subjecting it to ridicule; for those who should uphold the law are taken in by the pretty lies Casanova feeds them.

Casanova would like to believe that he has Bragadin completely under his spell. Yet it is Bragadin who shows him, in two instances, what true power means. Casanova incurs a gambling debt by pledging his word, and must repay Count Rinaldi or face dishonor. Bragadin assures him that he will take care of it, and he does not spend a penny of his own money to do so. The senator, who is a state authority, merely asks Rinaldi (a known cheater) to forgive Casanova's debt in writing (2: 202). On another occasion, Bragadin encourages his protégé to get a certain M. de l'Abadie, who is plotting to obtain a public office, to lend him some money; de l'Abadie, however, refuses Casanova's request. The next day, Bragadin goes to the senate and arranges that the office not be granted to de l'Abadie. Casanova understands (2: 205).

He knows full well that however successfully one might ridicule the law of the father, the imperatives of politics—that is, the all-powerful authority of the state—remain. He also knows, as he writes on the first page of this chapter, "that true liberty does not exist, nor can it exist anywhere" (2: 199). But for all of that, he does not abandon his dream of libertarian omnipotence. He will soon learn, at his own expense, that his subversion will never be more than a simulacrum, and that the Promethean position he covets is only tenable under circumstances of misprision or in a moment of madness. So what? he might answer, it was worth the try. And we would undoubtedly grant that it is initially because of Casanova's enterprise that his character fascinates us. For as we shall see, although he knows that failure awaits him, he will persist in pursuing this illusion and do everything in his power to make this chimera real, if only for an instant.

A few months later, he approaches a woman as she is getting off a ship from Ferrara. She is looking for her lover, who had fled after promising to marry her. Casanova learns that she is a countess; he hides her in the home of a widow and inquires into the whereabouts of this Venetian lover, who has vanished. For two weeks he lavishes his attentions on this young woman but never touches her. By a happy coincidence, her father comes to see M. Barbaro, one of Bragadin's friends, and asks for his aid in finding his daughter. This gives Casanova, who is busy shuttling between the widow's house and the senator's palace, a chance to bring out his numerical calculation and make it ask whether or not Barbaro should get involved in this matter. The oracle offers the singular response that Barbaro should only get involved "in order to persuade the count to forgive his daughter and abandon any idea of forcing her to marry the scoundrel, whom God had condemned to death" (2: 216–17).

Casanova is lucky, for if not actually dead, the runaway lover is "dead to the world, having taken a Capuchin's habit" (2: 222) because his mother had refused to pay his gambling debts and forced him to enter a monastery. But why did Casanova make the oracle say this? Casanova cares little whether this girl gets married or not, but he is most anxious to pursue his efforts to undermine paternity by returning this girl to her father, entirely submissive and absolutely virgin, after he has had his way with her. The proof of this is that although she is ready to give herself to him, he cannot sleep with the countess until he is assured of her father's clemency toward his daughter. One day, Casanova takes her in his arms, but brusquely gets up and leaves; as he writes, "I found myself so seized with the fear of obtaining what I did not think I yet deserved that my departure must have struck her as abrupt" (2: 218). In contrast, he faces no further obstacle once he meets the father and realizes that the man is ready to renounce marrying his daughter to the "scoundrel," and that he views Casanova as an honorable protector (2: 221); so Casanova spends the following night in the arms of the young countess (2: 222).

Throughout this transition episode, Casanova uses his usual ingredients. The first morning he returns to visit the countess, he sees her portrait on the dresser and laughs at "her whim of having herself painted as a man with black hair" (2: 213). But this is actually a portrait of her brother. When he meets the brother, Casanova thinks that he is the "living portrait of his sister" (2: 216) and finds him "as pretty as love" (2: 219). Yet that is not what allows him to carry out his quest; the important point—in which Casanova is truly innovative—is that he has simultaneously fooled the father by wearing the air of a generous chaperon, and rid himself of the daughter by placing her once again under her father's authority. He dupes the father even as he makes her return to the paternal aegis; he obeys the law of the father by enthusiastically transgressing it, and he presents this girl as a virgin he has never touched "and this is true virtue, which triumphs even in the midst of a lie" (2: 227). Casanova displays throughout this episode his usual impenitent irresponsibility, his very subtle and highly unstable mixture of submission to the rules, on the one hand, and of derision, on the other—a mélange of honor and fraud, or, as we saw much earlier, innocence and guilt, a combination so artful that the two elements become indistinguishable. It requires unfailing attention and the agility of a cat to persist in a state of misprision while steering clear of the usual well-beaten paths and producing, at one's own expense, the blindness that is necessary to succeed in love. Casanova lacks neither of these qualities.

At the beginning of the following year, he is strolling along a quay (2: 232) when he sees a pretty face in a passing gondola. He hails the gondola and gets on board, taking a seat across from a young girl named Christine and her uncle, a curate, who are returning to the countryside after having spent fifteen days in Venice in a futile attempt to find her a husband. A spontaneous conversation strikes up between a seducer who is growing more and more seduced and a free-spirited peasant girl who wants to enjoy herself but whose sole aim, finally, is to get married. Casanova joins in the game and even gets caught in it. He suggests that Christine come back to Venice and spend five or six months there so that he can get to know her, after which he will make her his wife. He believes himself to be sincere: "I would find a very honest family, where Christine's honor would be as safe as in a convent. . . . I saw that Christine was enchanted by this arrangement, and, sure that I would keep my word, I promised that everything would be arranged within eight days" (2: 242). The three travelers stop in Treviso. The curate is supposed to leave for two days, accompanied by Christine, and return with her to settle all the details; but because he is so pleased and confident in Casanova's good behavior, he leaves Christine with the young man. The following night, Casanova—who is sleeping in the same room as Christine—takes advantage of the situation and joins her in her bed, to marry her right away, as he puts it. Everything seems simple, the whole affair settled—on to the next.

That, however, is hardly the case. When the curate decides to leave Christine in Treviso, Casanova is speechless with surprise: "I was so astonished at this unexpected arrangement, made with such ease, that blood rushed to my head; I had a copious nosebleed for five to ten minutes, which did not alarm me at all, because this had happened to me before, but which did worry the curate, who feared that I was hemorrhaging. He went off to attend to his business, telling us that he would be back at nightfall" (2: 245).

We shall return to this untimely nosebleed. We can, at least, already deduce that the fear Casanova had felt in the presence of the young countess, when the promise of "happiness" entered into his romantic project, has shifted into a higher speed. There is a real danger to be faced here. To avoid it, Casanova has no other recourse than to commit himself more deeply and seriously to his promise of marriage. After spending a day with Christine, during which he does nothing but tell her stories, he concludes: "I was plotting in my head to marry her, having already decided to put her in the same house where I had kept the countess" (2: 246). It is only afterward that he is able to join Christine in her bed, but not without setting up another system of defense: "During this happy encounter, brought about purely by happenstance—and in which, because nothing had been premeditated, we could neither boast nor accuse ourselves of anything—we spent a few minutes absolutely unable to speak to each other" (2: 247).

In keeping with his well-practiced habit, Casanova must not bear any responsibility for what is going on here; he must absolve himself of all responsibility in order to erase any guilt. When he seduces this woman, he is an innocent who sincerely intends to marry her; he notes that he will have to obtain a dispensation if the wedding is to be held during Lent (2: 248).

But hardly has he set in place a strategy for respecting this woman and placing himself above suspicion than he grows pensive: "I saw that I had made a commitment that did not displease me; but I would have preferred that it not be so pressing. I could not avoid noticing that the first seeds of regret were sprouting in my loving, honest soul, and this made me sad. Yet I was sure that this lovely creature would never be made unhappy by my doing" (2: 248).

Casanova must therefore find a strategy that will allow him to get out of his fix while avoiding any dishonesty that could make him guilty. So he returns to Venice to convince his three friends that his "marriage had been written in the great book of destiny" (2: 249). Yet the very next day, he decides to "make Christine happy without marrying her" (2: 249). He embarks on a quest for a rare bird—"the perfect husband, one who would make her not only forgive my offenses against her, but also grow to bless me for tricking her and love me all the more for it" (2: 250). Casanova is decidedly not a Don Juan. He is incapable of making the women he deceives suffer—not so much for their sakes, of course, as for his own, for he cannot stand the thought that they might no longer love him. Each breakup must result in happiness for the other, so that, in going, he can preserve all of his self-esteem and lightheartedness, and thereby avoid the law and its tragic aspect.

How is he going to accomplish this? He turns once again to the cabala, which commands M. de Bragadin to ask Rome to grant the dispensation necessary for the wedding to be celebrated quickly. The cabala also tells M. Dandolo to find a young man, "handsome, wise, and fit to serve the Republic" (2: 251). Dandolo obliges by discovering a man named Charles who will do. Casanova announces "the change of scene" to Christine and introduces her to Charles, whom she accepts. The wedding takes place a few days later.

What is remarkable in this story is that Casanova had to promise to marry Christine to be able to sleep with her. This proves that the law of the father—of which the law of marriage is a mere variant—still has some power over him and that, deep down, his subversion has not really been carried out. Casanova is nonetheless cunning, in that he sincerely obeys this paternal law for just the amount of time needed to overcome his fear of women and then slips away. In this sense, he carries out his subversion after all, because far from using the law of the father to find his niche in the social network, he uses it purely to accomplish his ends of the moment. He thereby manages to benefit from all of the law's advantages without suffering any of its drawbacks. And he undermines the law all the more, because, according to his staging of the scene, the real marriage—between Christine and Charles—can take place not under the aegis of some well-established religion but only by virtue of the intervention of *Paralis* (2: 249), the spirit of Casanova expressed in the cabala.

We have yet to discuss the nosebleed that followed the announcement of a possible upcoming "happiness"—that is, the deflowering of a virgin. Casanova tells us that he was not alarmed, "because this had happened to [him] before" (2: 245). Now, the first mention of a nosebleed is made in the tale of his earliest childhood memory, recounted at the beginning of the *Memoirs*. We should examine this episode at length, because it seems to be the key to articulating Casanova's ties to magic, particularly his adventure with Javotte, which we shall read a bit later. At the age of eight years and four months, Casanova is struck with a violent nosebleed. His grandmother, who has raised him ever since his parents left for London when he was a year old, takes him to see a witch, who locks him in a trunk:

I hear someone laugh, cry, shout, sing, and hit the trunk by turns; it all means nothing to me. I am taken out of the trunk at last; my nose stops bleeding. After showering me with a hundred caresses, this extraordinary woman undresses me, puts me to bed, and burns some drug; she gathers the smoke in a sheet and wraps me in it, murmurs some spells over me, and finally unwraps me and gives me five very tasty candies to eat. (1: 4)

Then, under pain of death or of losing his blood, she orders him not to reveal any of these mysteries to anyone and promises him that he will be visited the next night by a charming lady, whom he should also keep secret. When he gets back to his grandmother's house, he goes to bed and falls asleep:

But when I awoke a few hours later, I saw or thought I saw a ravishing woman come down out of the chimney. . . . With a majestic, gentle air, she came slowly to sit on my bed; then she pulled some little boxes out of her pocket and emptied them on my head while murmuring a few words. After speaking to me at length about something that I did not understand in the least, she kissed me and left just as she had come; and afterward I went back to sleep. (1: 5)

Here is how the episode ends:

The next day, as soon as my grandmother came to my bedside to dress me, she ordered me not to say a word. She threatened me with death if I dared to repeat what must have happened to me during the night. It was because of this command—issued by the only woman who had an absolute author-

ity over me, and who had accustomed me to obey her every order blindly—
that I have always remembered this vision and placed it, tightly sealed, in
the most secret corner of my burgeoning memory.   (1: 5)

It would be well worth quoting at length all the reflections provoked by this memory; they show that Casanova is still caught in
this incident even if he attempts to rid himself of it. As he concludes, "It would be ridiculous to attribute my recovery to those
two extraordinary incidents; but it would also be wrong to say that
they did not play a role. As for the apparition of the beautiful
queen, I have always considered it a dream, unless someone staged
this masquerade for me on purpose" (1: 6).

This commentary, so typical of Casanova's attitude toward superstition and magic, clearly indicates that the visit to the witch and
her very effective spells are the source of Casanova's later behavior.
As an intelligent, sensible man, he cannot believe that these extravagances healed him; but as a patient now recovered, he cannot deny
some tie between these practices and the fact that his nose stopped
bleeding. For he must eventually find some way to explain the recovery: "Remedies for serious illnesses cannot always be found in
pharmacies. Every day, some phenomenon shows us how ignorant
we are. I believe that it is because of this that nothing is so rare as a
scholar whose mind is completely free of superstition" (1: 6). In a
word, Casanova feels compelled to draw this conclusion; because
his recovery has no rational explanation, he cannot help attributing
it to magic. One must in the end rely on one's judgment, at least
when interpreting something that occurs against a backdrop of
magic and superstition.

Casanova's nosebleed is actually ended by the combined effect of
the witch's shouts and gesticulations, the dream that follows, and
the secret imposed by the witch and his grandmother. These as-
sorted elements do not, however, play equivalent roles. The witch's
gestures obviously bring to mind rites of burial and birth; but because they are not in the least modified by a social context—unlike
the various initiation rites practiced in agrarian religions—they cannot be effective. In such traditional religions, these rites accomplish
what they symbolize by enacting a new integration of the group that
transforms the social status of the individual and thereby changes

his relation to himself. Here, in contrast, such rites draw their force from the fact that the witch is the grandmother's mediator. Because the grandmother believes in the power of spells to cure him, young Casanova must fulfill the wish of his grandmother—"the only woman who had an absolute authority over me"—and stop bleeding from his nose. Moreover, the vow of silence that the child must keep concerning this ceremony, and the death threat looming over him should he reveal it to anyone, make him react subjectively to the witch's action and structure his memory for the first time. Of course, for the witch, all of this is merely a precaution against the risk of being summoned before a tribunal, and charged with sorcery or the illegal practice of medicine because of a child's chattering. For Casanova, however, the effect is different: his life will be endangered unless he keeps to himself what he must forget for everyone else. For him, from this point on, repressing a secret will always be identified with staunching the flow of blood and, conversely, any loss of blood will signify that he has slipped in meeting his grandmother's desire.

It may be doubtful that the witch suspected any of this, but we should not exclude the possibility that the power held by these characters is rooted in some knowledge of the workings of the unconscious. Next to this woman, when Casanova practices magic, he will be nothing but a failed rationalist who imitates rituals yet lacks insight into things and beings. In any case, the witch's shrewdness is quite clear when she tells her young patient that he will be visited by a charming lady the next night. The fact that this child has nosebleeds must be related to women and their bleeding. And that is exactly what the dream says: "With a majestic, gentle air, she came slowly to sit on my bed; then she pulled some little boxes out of her pocket and emptied them on my head while murmuring a few words." To interpret the dream, we need only perform a few inversions. First, an inversion of the movement: instead of "pull from her pocket," we should read "put back in her pocket"; instead of "empty some little boxes," we should read "fill." Next, an inversion of the characters: it is Casanova, and not the woman, who, with his head or nose or penis, fills the little boxes and puts them into the woman's pockets. This is a dream about intercourse.

This dream is clearly much more effective in stopping the flow of blood than the rites performed by the witch (representative of the grandmother's wishes), who shifts the emphasis from the child to the woman. The identification with women manifested in the nosebleed is resolved in a dream through a sexual relation, desired by the figure who represents the grandmother, who herself represents Casanova's mother. This is undoubtedly the source of Casanova's passion for seduction, for he shall never desist in his effort to transform his dream into reality—that is, he shall devote himself to repeating the act of intercourse with every woman possible in order to save himself from this early identification. It is also the source of Casanova's desire to pass from one sex to another, his passion for confusing genders, which we have so frequently witnessed. In this context, however, it is easy to understand that if a particular kind of sexual experience did not protect him from identifying with women but instead thrust him into identifying with them once again, it would be considered dangerous, even impossible. And that is exactly what happens when Casanova sets out to deflower a virgin: the predictable appearance of blood not only nullifies the liberating effect of the intercourse, but also turns sex into the opposite of what it should be, because it leads directly to what Casanova was trying to avoid. Yet at the same time, the act of deflowering virgins becomes Casanova's supreme fascination— because he fears it, of course, but more important, because opposites come together in this act: pain and its remedy are superimposed, and Casanova's identification with women is both expressed and overcome.

The last scene of the episode ensures that the preceding events will be effective. When he awakens, the dreamer is ordered to keep silent. Casanova emphasizes that this unspoken message, which contains both a death threat and his grandmother's wish, marked the beginning of his memory. Before this tale, he had stated that "in early August, 1733, my faculty of memory developed" (1: 4); and later, "it was because of this command . . . that I have always remembered this vision and placed it, tightly sealed, in the most secret corner of my burgeoning memory" (1: 5). For him, this silence will have the effect of a primal scene. Because of the secret he must keep, the event becomes Casanova's first recollection, that is, the memory that hides and reveals the primitive form of Casanova's psychic functioning; in other words, the memory in which a phantasm—the crucible of Casanova's entire life story—is transposed after the fact, with all the necessary adjustments. Casanova takes care to warn us that "many things become real that only existed beforehand in our imagination" (1: 6). The young Casanova is caught in an event/recollection/tale that bears the seal of the woman who held an absolute authority. Nothing that he will do later will be anything but a repetition of this, in one of many variations.

We are ready, at this point, to read the strange story recounted at the end of the second volume and the beginning of the third. While passing through Mantua in 1748, Casanova goes to visit a local luminary who has a collection of objects that he claims to be quite ancient, including a knife purportedly used by Saint Peter to cut off Malchus's ear (John 18: 10). Casanova enters into a true delirium, perfectly described by a conversation too long to quote here. He then suggests using the knife (whose sheath is to be recovered) to unearth buried treasures. It seems that just such a treasure is located not far from there in Cesena, under the property of a peasant. Casanova takes up residence in this peasant's home and begins preparations for a grand magic ceremony designed to uncover the treasure, all the while gracing Javotte, the oldest daughter, with his attentions. The plan is carried out to perfection up to the moment when—just as the "magic" is about to take effect, the treasure appear, and Javotte lose her virginity—a storm breaks that startles the magician; petrified with fear, he returns to his room, and discreetly leaves the next day.

What is initially striking in this unbelievably extravagant tale is the fascination that overtakes Casanova upon seeing the knife, made sacred by the collector's credulity; with an astonishing, revealing speed, Casanova himself is drawn into this fascination, even if he uses it in passing to denounce the owner's stupidity. There is something in the plan he sets up to dupe this man that overwhelms him, and that he cannot but suspect, although he documents the events well enough to make an interpretation possible. If he were not deeply caught up in the story, how could we explain the price he pays for this knife and his feverish efforts to fabricate a sheath for it from an old shoe sole in the middle of the night? And how could we explain why the mere sight of the knife immediately reminds him of these words of Christ's: "Mitte gladium tuum in vaginam" (2: 293; John 18: 11)? Let us say from the outset that, as events will prove, Casanova is excited because, for him, this instrument represents both a penis and castration; it is, therefore, urgently necessary that he find a vagina.

Such interpretations may be abusive, yet we see that the action develops in two directions: the uncovering of a hidden treasure by means of the famous knife, and the deflowering of a virgin. Penetration of the earth and of the woman are obviously one and the same act reproducing the use of the sheath in the most transparent registers. Because they are so transparent, however, Casanova's various undertakings will be melded into one failure. The link between these two versions of the same act is constantly underscored: "I sorely regretted having pledged to postpone the great sacrifice [deflowering] until the night the treasure was to be unearthed" (2: 303); and, as Casanova says to Javotte, "The full success of our operation [digging up the treasure] depends solely on the pleasure that you can feel in my presence, barring all constraints" (2: 303). Similarly, after his failure, he tells Javotte that "because her innocence was not necessary for uncovering the treasure, she was free to marry if the opportunity arose" (3: 5). First, Casanova exploits a very old tradition according to which the deflowering of a virgin must be performed by a sacred person; he has a ceremonial gown made for him to wear on the big night and refers to that event as "the great sacrifice" (2: 301). In doing this, he is clearly identifying with those who overcome the fear of castration and thereby master it, to some extent. Second, he refuses to arouse Javotte's love, demanding instead that she be obedient and submissive so that he can wield an absolute authority (2: 300). It is as if he feared that this authority would be watered down were he to try to seduce her through love, for love would shield her eyes (and his own) from the real difficulty of the undertaking: proving his omnipotence, that is, his absolute non-castration. He seems to be saying: the threat of castration will no longer exist for me if I can over-come my fear of deflowering a virgin in a magical, non-amorous context.

It is impossible for Casanova to dissociate this effort from the extraction of the treasure by means of the marvelous knife. Yet he would indeed like to distinguish the two: "For relief from the heat, she [Javotte] stripped herself naked, and then fell asleep. I did the same, but I sorely regretted having pledged to postpone the great sacrifice until the night the treasure was to be unearthed. I knew that the operation was bound to fail; but I also knew that it would not be because I had spoiled her virginity" (2: 303).

To perform the great sacrifice would not have ruined the attempt to dig up the treasure, because this operation was bound to fail from the start; yet during this period of preparations, Casanova fails to take advantage of the young girl, choosing instead, as he says, to "respect the sanctuary" (2: 303). What holds him back in this in-stance is surely not his commitment to any of these gullible fools, but something else, which is clearly expressed after the famous night that the storm hits:

I gathered up the circle, and, after commanding the two friends to retire in silence, I went to my room, where I took one look at Javotte and found her so pretty that she frightened me. I let her dry me off without looking at her and told her in a pitiful tone to go get into her bed. She told me the next day that when she saw me trembling despite the heat of the season, I frightened her.

After a total of eight hours, I felt sick of this farce. When Javotte ap-peared before me, I was astonished to find that she seemed completely changed. Her gender no longer seemed different from my own, because I no longer considered my gender different from hers. A powerfully super-stitious idea led me to believe that this girl's innocent state was protected, and that I would have been struck dead had I dared to attack it. (3: 3)

A real impostor would have taken out his failure as a magician on Javotte. But Casanova cannot do that, because his failure—which he had known in advance without wanting to acknowledge it—does not remove him from the scene he had staged, but rather plunges him into it at a level that is no longer mere theater. He is sick of this farce because it is no longer a farce for him. In reality, he has always been afraid of Javotte; she was always "an object of horror" (3: 4) in his view, and it is for this reason that she frightens him now. His clowning around only serves to restore his confidence in the face of this taboo character. His antics do not always perform the function he had expected, because they are too close to their symbolic transparence and tend to undo the castration threat too clearly. The masquerade is not related to any real powers, so it changes into its opposite. Rather than appearing to be the high priest, master of woman and earth, he comes to be identical to the woman, his gender no longer different from hers; in his madness, he sees himself as truly castrated. The farce fails because his imposture is pushed beyond all limits. Far from protecting and blinding him as in other circumstances, the farce becomes the means by which his oft-repeated project is brutally revealed.

To speak, therefore, of Casanova as an impostor or as a person who falls for his own scam does not account for what underlies the episode: a truly Promethean effort to save the penis from any threat of castration, an effort whose condition and culmination were to have been an absolute deflowering, devoid of love. Magic allowed him to claim to be omnipotent by invoking the aid of a supernatural force. In all of his escapades, Casanova is quite serious; he knows that the perforation of a hymen is not a surgical matter, that it cannot occur without casting some "spells" and tracing out some cabalistic "characters" in the sand (3: 1). We should consider Casanova not merely as an impostor, but as an impostor who recognizes that if one wants to overcome the fear of virginity—or, more generally speaking, the fear of women—one must appeal to some reality that transcends instinct. His failure is not fully accounted for if we see no more in it than the discomfiture of an unmasked con man. Rather, it stems from the project itself: to take on the taboo of virginity and the threat of castration directly, without recourse either to love or to any form of submission.

All of these chapters are infused with the same wish to affirm his omnipotence. With Bragadin, Casanova undertakes to use the cabala to overpower the father, thereby subverting obedience to paternal law. After using the cabala in various amorous adventures (an apparent testing of his power over the destinies of these women),

Casanova gets the idea of taking it much further. His nosebleed in the presence of Christine reminds him of the highly effective methods used by the witch when he was a child. So at the earliest opportunity, he attempts a much more radical subversion: undermining the symbolic order that oversees the exchange of women, to show that he is able to do without it by transgressing the virginity taboo, an act that would have proved his omnipotence over women. His failure is on the measure of his fantastic ambitions: he finds himself, in the end, identical to a woman.

Le Plus Honnête Homme au Monde
[The Greatest Gentleman in the World]

CASANOVA pretends to forget his misadventure. In Cesena, he re-
sumes his old habits of gambling and going to the opera. Yet despite this, he senses that he should not linger too long in this region,
for the whiff of magic is still not greatly appreciated in high places:
"A slight fear of the Inquisition persisted in haunting me, and I already
felt as if I had informers hot on my heels" (3: 6). So he decides to
leave for Naples, the city in which Fortune had always smiled on
him, where he had brought his journey through horror to a definitive end, and where he might meet up again with his old flames
Bellino-Thérèse and Donna Lucrezia. For he must recover from the
wound reopened by Javotte's virginity, which even a particularly
well-developed faculty of forgetting may not heal. Henriette will
do this for him. Thanks to a stroke of luck and, undoubtedly, his
own incomparable intuition, Casanova will find in Henriette the
medicine that he so urgently needs at this time.

One morning, he hears a great ruckus in the inn where he is staying. Some policemen, called in by the innkeeper, have burst into
the room next to his in order to arrest a Hungarian officer who is
there with a woman who may not be his wife. Casanova intervenes,
moved by "the honesty of his soul, which could not bear to see a
foreigner treated in this manner," but also by the curiosity aroused
by this woman, whom he has never seen (3: 14). After Casanova
appeals to the bishop and general of the region, the incident is re-

solved and official apologies are extended. As usual, Casanova is especially excited that this person is dressed as an officer and re-ferred to as a man; so he decides to go off with the two officers to Parma, where they must report. He will first serve as an interpreter, because the Hungarian can make himself understood only in Latin in this region, and the woman knows only French, which her com-panion does not understand.

During their journey, it does not take Casanova long to realize that the solidarity of this couple, made up of a fifty-five-year-old Magyar and a thirty-year-old Frenchwoman, is not unbreachable. He therefore asks the Hungarian officer whether he would agree to leave Henriette (that is the name the woman goes by) with him when they arrive in Parma. The Hungarian, who must return to his country but who likes Henriette well enough not to abandon her friendless, readily accepts the proposition. Casanova then dis-cusses the matter with Henriette and asks her to choose: either he will go to Parma with her and she will be his entirely, or he will leave her immediately. After making fun of his menacing tone, she answers, "Yes, come to Parma" (3: 36). Thus she accompanies him to Parma and spends three months there before disappearing to re-turn to France, without ever telling him who she is and why she came to Italy.

But who, then, is this strange woman who passes so easily from one man to another without breaking her silence about her real name and story? All that Casanova learns from the Hungarian offi-cer is that he had met her first in Civitavecchia and then in Rome, where she had joined him in his carriage as he was about to depart for Parma. The officer had been told in advance that they would go their separate ways when they reached this city. She later explains to Casanova that, while in Rome, she had escaped from her father-in-law, who wanted to cloister her in a convent. Why? Casanova will never know. Yet it is with this woman that he will spend an idyll of rare peace and happiness that might well have lasted longer had she not decided to leave as matter-of-factly as she had chosen to go with him to Parma and stay there, protected from curious stares.

Indeed, all that she asks is to live secretly in a city where she is unknown. Although she goes to Parma incognito, she must not go out, for fear that she might meet an old acquaintance; that, however, is exactly what happens. Casanova has a very low tolerance for the life of a recluse; so to make him happy, she agrees to go to the opera, and then to accept an occasional invitation to appear in polite society. One day, a certain M. d'Antoine believes that he recognizes her, although she herself has no idea who he might be. This gentleman is connected to Henriette's family and thus succeeds in arranging a meeting with her, which Casanova is asked not to attend. M. d'Antoine serves as a mediator between Henriette and her family; and after prolonged negotiations (whose subject remains a mystery to Casanova), she decides to return to France. Casanova accompanies her all the way to Geneva, where she asks him never to try to see her again, or to let on that he knows her should their paths cross by chance. He will in fact meet her again in Aix-en-Provence in 1763 and 1769, that is, fourteen and twenty years after their idyll; but, oddly enough, he does not recognize her. He will later correspond with her for more than twenty years; these letters, however, have disappeared, for Casanova vowed not to publish them until after the death of this woman, who remains an exceptional figure among all of the women mentioned in the *Memoirs*.

In the words of Félicien Marceau, "Henriette is one of Casanova's fondest memories."* J. Rives Childs goes further: "Perhaps no woman so captivated Casanova as Henriette; few women obtained so deep an understanding of him. She penetrated his outward shell early in their relationship, resisting the temptation to unite her destiny with his. She came to discern his volatile nature, his lack of social background, and the precariousness of his finances. Before leaving, she slipped into his pocket 500 louis, mark of her evaluation of him." And later, Rives Childs remarks: "Henriette, that captivating creature who had made the deepest impression on him of all the countless women he had known," and again, "No woman ever touched his heart so deeply as this member of the nobility of Aix."† For, according to Rives Childs, Henriette's real name is Jeanne-Marie d'Albert de Saint-Hippolyte, born in 1718 and wed in

---

* *Une Insolente Liberté: les aventures de Casanova* (Gallimard, 1983), p. 112.

† *Casanova: A Biography Based on New Documents* (London: Allen and Unwin, 1961), pp. 60, 172, 243.

1744 (five years before meeting Casanova) to Jean-Baptiste-Laurent Boyer de Fonscolombe.

Casanova is not taken in by first impressions. When she gives up her military attire and, in a dress, receives her two admirers, they are awestruck:

The door opened at last, and there she was. She received us with a lovely curtsy, made with an unaffected air that had none of the imposing tone, none of the gaiety of military free-spiritedness. 'Twas we who were surprised and disconcerted by her new appearance. She had us sit next to her: she looked at the captain amiably and at me with loving tenderness, but without any of the easy familiarity that a young officer can express without degrading his love, which would not be suitable in a lady of status. This new bearing forced me to join the game without seeming to, for Henriette was not playing a role. She was actually the persona she was presenting. (3: 51)

He notes several times the exact propriety of this woman's reactions, always steady, never over- or underdone: "Henriette, to whom I had not said a thing in advance, looked at everything on the table with an expression of great satisfaction, but made no demonstration save for expressing her pleasure by praising the high quality of the items that I had chosen with such care. There was no greater mirth because of this, no unseemly thanks or expressions of gratitude" (3: 41–42).

Henriette certainly fulfills his long-cherished wish to possess a great lady. What he was unable to accomplish with Marquise G. in Rome or with Mme F. in Corfu (and will not, it seems, obtain in Paris from the duchess of Chartres) he obtains here from this utterly unaffected woman.

There are, of course, many other reasons that explain why Henriette becomes one of his fondest memories. As he exclaims in a soliloquy, "So who is this girl, who mixes the most noble sentiment with an outer appearance of extreme libertinage?" (3: 29). To describe her "most noble sentiment," Casanova affirms that she is "beautiful, witty, and cultivated" (3: 50) and goes so far as to say: "The joy that was flooding my soul was even greater when I was conversing with her during the day than when I held her in my arms at night" (3: 49). That must not have happened to him very often.

As for her apparent libertinage, he deduces it from the fact that it did not require any pleading for her to give herself to the Hungarian officer, and that she was passed over to Casanova, certainly with no vulgarity, but with no great resistance either. Moreover, the officer's uniform she is wearing when she meets Casanova for the first time is perhaps more than a simple mask donned in order to accompany a military man with greater ease, for everyone recognizes that she is a woman. Casanova may already be suggesting her varied proclivities. In 1763, he passes through Aix with Marcoline, his mistress at the time, and they are invited to spend the night in a chateau; the countess of the chateau, their hostess—who will turn out to be Henriette—wastes no time in taking Marcoline into her bed. Here is how Casanova relates the anecdote: "I could see from the kisses they gave each other that they were in agreement; all that I said to the countess upon bidding her good night was that I could not guarantee the gender of the person she was taking to bed. She answered quite clearly that 'she could only gain from it'" (9: 82).

If we recall the phantasms seen time and time again in Casanova's romantic practices, we could conclude that two factors are decisive in attracting him to Henriette. First, beyond her disguise, there is her double sexual practice, which is not displayed openly until later but is certainly present from the start. Second, there is the secrecy surrounding her identity. As her lover, Casanova never knows with whom he is dealing, and their later encounters—in which she goes unrecognized twice—only underscore this fact. Our hero of noncommitment always manages to (mis)take Henriette for someone else, seeing the woman before him without ever recognizing her.

However necessary these two factors undoubtedly are for setting in motion Casanova's romantic machine, they would not have been enough at this point to liberate our sorcerer from his failure with Javotte, a recollection that comes back to haunt him several times during the first days of his liaison with Henriette. This woman is not the least bit coquettish or affected. With an ease and wit that never fail her, she says exactly what she thinks and only what she wants. Even when in love, she does not abandon her lucidity for a second. With her, Casanova is forced to give up his masquerade and the juggling acts he believes he needs in order to dazzle. He is reduced to a kind of frankness for which he has no talent, and which makes him rather clumsy. When he declares his love for her and asks her to choose—"Either I possess you entirely or I shall stay here, and let you go on to Parma with the officer" (3: 34)—she mocks him gently: "Forgive me for laughing, I beg of you, for never in my life did I ever imagine such a furious declaration of love. Do you know what it means to tell a woman in a love declaration, which should be tender, 'Madame, one or the other, choose this instant'?" (3: 35). And when he continues in this tone, she adds, "Do you know that you seem angry?" (3: 36). When he shows himself for what he is and asks his companion to do the same, it is because, in his obsession with penetration, he can feel the ground giving way under his feet. He absolutely must be realistic when faced with someone who is frank from the start; he feels the need to unmask and be unmasked, to be just what he is, with no make-up or finery, without casting "spells" or "tracing letters." Henriette is the woman who dispenses with all that is shadowy or glittery, the better to return to what is safe and solid: "My dear friend, you spend a great deal of money on me, and if you spend it in order to make me love you more, it is as good as thrown away, for I do not love you any more than I did the day before yesterday. Everything that you do could only please me, because I see more and more how worthy you are of love; but I have no need for such a conviction" (3: 44).

After meeting Casanova in 1763 without revealing her identity, she sends him this simple note: "To the *plus honnête homme* I know in the world," signed only "Henriette" (9: 86). This note is a way of telling Casanova that she has no further doubt about his character, which she could not trust fourteen years beforehand. As Félicien Marceau writes,

Yet even if the expression *honnête homme* has evolved since the eighteenth century, I think that one can detect in it a mark of surprise—a pleasant surprise, for that matter; I would even call it a certificate. It is as if Henriette were grateful to Casanova for having maintained a reserve toward her, a discretion on which she might not have counted in Parma. Let us recall that, in Parma, despite their liaison of several months, she never revealed her name to him. The episode of the Croix d'Or [their encounter in 1763] proves that she did not tell him her address either; that is, she left him with no means of tracking her down. Finally, in her letter of 1769, when she promises to recount "the whole story behind our meeting in Cesena" (11: 181), she indicates clearly that she had told him nothing about this matter in Parma. Was her secret so heavy at the time? I would tend instead to think that, at that moment and whatever he might say, Casanova was not yet adept at creating illusions, and that, behind the attentive lover, Countess Henriette (like little Countess A.S.) detected a man who was not of her class—perhaps an adventurer or a young fool capable of committing some stupidity, a man whom, in any case, she could not entirely trust. *

With her, for her, Casanova throws off all traces of imposture. And he needed urgently to do this after the outlandish tale of the knife and its sheath, in order to chase out the phantoms in his mind that had led him to such a state of terror. At least once in his life, the enamored libertine did not have to put on an act for a woman— more important, he did not have to put one on for himself. He saves this moment of truth, this gift proffered by Henriette, as something precious, as his sole means of preserving within himself a trait that would allow him some modicum of self-respect. This is undoubt- edly the reason that, to the great astonishment of his biographers, he is unable to recognize her, because something very precious within him forbids it. If he had recognized her, he would have lost the title of *plus honnête homme*, which no one else could grant him, especially not himself, except of course when he is trying to justify his most ingenious scams. He could have told Henriette: you are the most fascinating woman I have ever met because, thanks to you, one day I had no wish to disguise myself.

Yet there is another trait in Henriette that seduces him. Because she understands immediately that it would horrify him, she never once reveals anything about her destiny to him. There is no ques- tion that this thirty-year-old woman, who has fled her country and her family and finds herself with no resources, is in the midst of a crisis. She is able to keep from confiding this to anyone, which might have eased her burden somewhat. With other women, Casanova would have been (and will be) prompt to feel pity, but this pity quickly weighs on him and becomes the harbinger of a break, nec- essary for him to regain his liberty. Yet Henriette does not arouse any such sentiments in him. Not only does she not use her situation

---

* *Une Insolente Liberté*, pp. 114–15.

to move him, not only does she not exploit him, but she does not ask anything of him. She even repays him generously for what he has spent on her: she owes him nothing. It is easy to understand why he never feels threatened in the face of such a woman, never feels the need to deploy the instruments of an escape. He can submit to her (3: 34, 37) without losing any of his lightheartedness. This brings him great happiness, for during their liaison he is not called upon to exercise the responsibility he so abhors. With her, he is like an innocent, perhaps like a child.

Henriette is an exception in the story of Casanova's love life because she artfully combines two sets of parameters that seem mutually exclusive for him. Because she maintains ambiguity about her own gender, and mystery about her name, she protects him from the fearful panic of having to differentiate, which would deprive him of his childish sense of omnipotence. Because she forces him to step down off the stage and absolves him of all responsibility, he is both obliged and able to speak the language of frankness and discretion. In a word, she allows him to reconcile his passion for misprision and his penchant for sincerity. With her, he has no need to construct complicated defensive scenarios to temper the violence triggered within him by the sight of a woman, for she herself fabricates the illusion he cannot do without. He is able to forgo dazzling and being bedazzled, for she has veiled her identity herself. She gives him peace and happiness, if only for a moment, for, as a woman, she never reveals herself.

He is not, for all that, completely cured of the terror brought on in part by his inventions as a pseudo–magician and even more so by his wish to transgress the taboo of virginity. He will need a great deal more time to do that. We have reached 1749 in the *Memoirs*. It will not be until 1753 that Casanova has another love affair worth mentioning. Between these two dates, he will only have women whom he pays or who offer themselves to him (3: 172). As for virgins, he has become incapable of deflowering them. While in Paris, he makes the acquaintance of a Mlle Vesian, who would love to latch on to him. As he writes, "I not only never tried anything with her, but promised myself that I would not be the first to put her on the wrong track" (3: 181). For although "she had never strayed from the straight and narrow path," she "did not play the prude" (3: 183). Casanova explains the fact that he never "reaches a resolution" on this matter by invoking his refusal to get attached. But as he acknowledges a few lines later: "It was three hours after midnight when I bid Mlle Vesian farewell; since she naturally could not assume that my restraint was the effect of my virtue, she must have attributed it either to shame, or to impotence, or to some secret illness" (3: 184).

His secret illness is all the less secret because this young lady will no longer be inaccessible to him once she has been seduced and abandoned a few days afterward by the young count of Narbonne. Pity succeeds in arousing him and moves him to find her a position as a well-established dancer, so that he can get her off of his hands.

The same obstacle arises before him a short while later. He is attracted to the sister of an Irish actress named Morfi, who is perfectly willing to give up her virginity for a price: "I found the little Morfi ready to let me do whatever I wanted with her, except what I had no desire to do" (3: 197). Money cannot serve as a pretext, as he admits: "The older Morfi thought that I was the biggest dupe ever, because in two months I had spent 300 francs for nothing. She attributed that to my greed. What greed! I spent six louis to have the girl painted stark naked in a lifelike pose by a German painter" (3: 198). This woman is not destined to be his, either. The portrait makes its way right to Louis XV, who orders it to be brought and installed at Versailles. The older sister, who is baffled by all of this, interrogates Casanova:

"Is it possible, my dear friend, that you left her a virgin? Tell me the truth."

"If she was before, I can assure you that she did not cease to be so on my account."

"Certainly she was, for I gave her to no one but you. Ah! The honest man! She was destined for the king. Who could have predicted it! I admire your virtue. Come here and let me kiss you." (3: 200)

This time, however, the terms "honnête homme" and "virtue" do not ring as true as they did coming from Henriette's pen. Casanova is in the grips of a truly insurmountable fear. How will he resolve it?

The Quadrille

C ASANOVA will attempt to overcome his fear of virginity by undertaking a series of clever scenarios that are novel only in their intensity. His years in Paris (from June 1750 to October 1752), a flurry of frivolity and wit, do nothing to ease his troubled spirit. He will therefore have to take up the question again, from scratch, and return to Venice via Metz, Frankfurt, and Dresden; it is now May 1753.

Casanova knows full well that he is grappling with the same question and must therefore retrace his old tracks; but if he is to follow the same old path, he wants to do it at a different pace this time. He finds everything just as he had left it, as if his journey had done him no good whatsoever; and it is in this vein that he begins this new chapter:

I was delighted to find myself back in the city of my birth, for a man is always partial to his home; and now that I surpassed many of my peers in experience and knowledge of the laws of honor and polite manners, I was eager to take up my old habits, but more methodically this time, and with greater reserve. I was pleased to see that in the study where I used to sleep and write, my papers were covered with dust, a sure sign that no one had gone in there for three years.   (3: 233)

After making this declaration that he is going to take up his old habits, "more methodically this time, and with greater reserve," he bids farewell to his journeys and his disappointing love affairs by returning a miniature portrait he had filched from an actress in Vienna as revenge for her refusing his advances (3: 234).

To lend a solemn touch to the inauguration of a new era in his life, Casanova mentions four times in the first pages of this chapter the grandiose ceremony held each year on Ascension Day, during which the doge of Venice comes to "marry the Adriatic Sea" (2: 233). We might think that this is an insignificant detail, but surely it is not; for Casanova's new method of overcoming his fear of virginity will lead him not only to promise marriage, as he did with Christine, but to do everything in his power to go through with it.

I would like to make a brief digression here, both to express my admiration for the work of Casanova scholars and to suggest that their perplexity over a chronological difficulty posed by this chapter is related to certain literary problems that can be resolved by paying close attention to its composition. The dilemma revolves around the date to be assigned to the event of the "wedding of the sea." Casanova claims to have arrived in Venice two days before Ascension Day in 1753 (3: 232). He says elsewhere, however, that in this particular year, the wedding between Venice and the sea had to be postponed until the following Sunday because of bad weather. Now according to Bruno Brunelli, who is quoted in a footnote to the Brockhaus edition (3: 341), the ceremony took place exactly on Ascension Day in 1753 and 1754; but it was in fact delayed until Sunday in 1748. We also know from "an official document issued by the office of the notary Manzoni pertaining to some false bills of exchange" (3: 342) that in 1748 Casanova was acquainted with Pier Capretta, the brother of C.C., who will be central to this chapter. The Livre de poche edition of the *Memoirs* confirms these facts and juxtaposes the chronology of the events of 1753 with another chronology outlining the events of 1748. The Pléiade edition settles the issue in a very different way: "Casanova could not have arrived in Venice before February 1754, as several convergent clues prove"— clues that are not presented to the reader. And later: "Casanova is mistaken; the wedding with the sea took place on May 31, 1753, and May 23, 1754, both Ascension Days."* The Brockhaus edition

* *Mémoires* (Le Livre de poche, Gallimard, 1967), 3: 334; *Mémoires* (Bibliothèque de la Pléiade, Gallimard, 1964), 1: 1190.

tries instead to redeem the historical precision of the *Memoirs*: "Casanova may have met C.C.'s brother a second time in 1753 (but it would be difficult to believe that the episode with C.C. discussed in the subsequent chapters could have occurred in 1748)" (3: 341). The latest (partial) edition of the *Memoirs*, which probably jumps to conclusions rather hastily, is nonetheless the only one to leave room for a literary interpretation without dwelling too much upon the exactitude of the events: "The wedding was reported in 1748, not in 1753. Casanova seems to transpose his encounter with P.C. and his sister C.C. to the later date."* For one can convincingly argue (as J. Rives Childs implies) that Casanova does not make a mistake or confuse events, but actually transposes—that is, he composes: he is careful to account for history, but relegates it to a position of secondary importance to other concerns.† If he makes a point of noting that the wedding was postponed in 1753, whereas the postponement actually occurred in 1748, might he not be suggesting that, for reasons immanent to his story, he wants to conflate his two stays in Venice into one?

If one can, as I hope, demonstrate that Casanova's behavior with C.C. is perfectly consistent with 1753—that is, with this moment in the *Memoirs*—then it follows that the author had to assemble in one chapter everything that pertains to this intrigue; in this case, that he may actually have met Pier Capretta, C.C.'s brother, in 1748, would be irrelevant. By mentioning the wedding of Venice and the sea four times, Casanova is able to use the passages between each mention to introduce elements that will later serve as a point of departure for a tale of promised marriage. As for Pier Capretta, a crook who wants to sell his sister, it is crucial that he be introduced here, in 1753, for he serves as a foil to our hero, who no longer wants to be or can be a seducer, pure and simple; however, as we shall see, Capretta's character also foreshadows Casanova's joust with Cardinal de Bernis, which is first suggested by Casanova's dealings with Capretta. It would certainly be an error to think that the *Memoirs* were written carelessly. Not only do we have, in certain cases, several versions of the same event at our disposal—

* *Mémoires, 1744–1756* (Garnier-Flammarion, 1977), p. 647.
† *Casanova: A Biography Based on New Documents* (London: Allen and Unwin, 1961), pp. 76–77.

indicating that Casanova is truly engaged in composition—but one could hardly attribute the implacable internal logic of his life story and love affairs to mere happenstance. Others have suggested my point: might not the *Memoirs* also be a novel, a life transformed into an authentic tragic tale, its facts changed into the scenes of a tragicomedy?

In any case, the staging of the scene is meticulous in this chapter. Whereas the first mention of the wedding of the sea serves to erase the past, the second mention introduces the figure of Fortune, the happenstance that Casanova would like to invoke so as to appear a victim or pawn: "If I had left Padua ten seconds before, or after, everything that happened in my life would have been different; if it is true that destiny depends upon combinations, I would have had another destiny. The reader will judge of that. So, because I left Padua at this *fatal* moment . . ." (3: 234–35). Along the way, a few feet from his carriage, a tilbury overturns toward the river, * and a woman who is accompanying an officer seems on the verge of falling in; Casanova rushes to save her.

There is a third mention of the wedding of the sea. Casanova is masked; a passing woman taps him on the shoulder with her fan. After the fourth mention, this woman reveals that it is she whom he had saved from the tipped tilbury, and they begin flirting with each other. But the scene changes, and it is the officer, this lady's lover, who takes center stage. He proposes that Casanova join him in some rather sordid financial negotiations. Casanova declines, but the officer senses the true character of the man he has solicited and introduces him to his sister, hoping to get some money in the process. This sister is Catterina Capretta, who is never called anything but C.C. in the *Memoirs*. Everything is in its place: "I left this house sad and dreamy, overly affected by the rare qualities I had discovered in this girl. I vowed never to see her again. I cursed myself for not being the kind of man who could ask her father for her hand in marriage. She seemed the perfect woman to make me happy" (3: 241).

The tale of the adventure is interrupted here for a moment—but not by just anything. Casanova has to retrace the itinerary he had

---

* A tilbury is a light, two-wheeled carriage.

followed during his youth in Venice and succeed at everything in which he had failed, to mark distinctly that he has entered a new era. The starting point is the house of Mme Manzoni (3: 241), a sort of kindly mother who had always smiled at his youthful follies and never took seriously his resolutions to remain true to a particular profession. It is in her home that he had always found a refuge. Thanks to this woman, he sees Thérèse Imer once again, "the Thérèse for whom I had suffered a caning from old Senator Malipiero thirteen years before" (3: 241). At that time the caning served to chastise his attempt to prove his difference; but this time he is not interrupted and succeeds in making love to her.

Not long after his misadventure with Malipiero, he had had a dispute with Abbé Grimani, entrusted with the task of selling the furniture of the family home. Casanova now succeeds in paying Grimani off so that he will offer an inheritance to Casanova's brother. Here again, he erases a past failure.

Finally, after making a second visit to C.C., he meets the count of Bonafede, whose daughter Casanova had found so attractive at Fort Saint-André, but whom he could not bring himself to approach later because of her misery and dirtiness. Once again, he is able to correct this bad memory. He goes to the count's residence, where he is received by the young countess, now elegantly attired, "lovely and vivacious": "The torrent of kisses, which were exchanged and returned out of pure friendship at first, overtook our senses so quickly that the event that customarily should only take place at the end of the visit, occurred within the first fifteen minutes" (3: 244).

Everything is ready now for Casanova, who has regained his strength by settling his accounts with the past, to throw himself into a new romantic adventure. What is striking in this episode is his oft-repeated refrain that he does not want to deceive his beloved C.C. Before obtaining "the ultimate favors," he does not make her any promises that he does not plan to keep afterward. This time, he does not follow his usual scenario of blinding himself in order to obtain his ends, only to promptly regain his lucidity and beat a hasty retreat. He perseveres. This is an astonishing change in his behavior, which we also observed with Henriette—that is, after Javotte. This change is translated here by the theme of marriage, which pervades all of their conversations. It is only through talk of marriage in fact that they can express or suppress their love. During the first visit: "I cursed myself for not being the kind of man who could ask her father for her hand in marriage" (3: 241). During the second: "Three hours of pure discussion, which flew by very quickly for me, left me so enamored that I could see I was incurable. Upon taking my leave, I told her that I envied the good fortune of the man whom heaven had chosen for her" (3: 243). During their next encounter, it is C.C. who speaks in this register: "Even my mother says that one cannot be fooled in these matters, and that you are surely one of the most honest boys in Venice. And what is more, you are not married. That was the first thing I asked my brother. Do you remember telling me that you envied the good fortune of the man who would have me as his wife? At that very moment I was telling myself that the woman who will have you will be the happiest girl in Venice" (3: 247).

We hear the same refrain when they find themselves alone together in the garden on Giudecca. While reading this dialogue, one might laugh at the farce they are both playing; yet this passage is indeed necessary to maintain the tone of the chapter and show that Casanova is no longer the same with women. Obviously, the conversation is still a bit forced:

"My beloved friend," I asked her, while holding her tightly in my arms, "are you sure that I love you? Do you think me capable of failing you? Are you certain that you would never regret marrying me?"

"I am more than certain, my dear heart; I will never believe you capable of making me unhappy."

"Then let us marry this very minute before God, in his presence; we could not have a more loyal, respectable witness than our Creator, who knows our consciences and the purity of our intentions. We do not need any documents. Let us pledge ourselves to each other, and join our destinies right now, and make each other happy. We will have the Church ceremony when everything can be made public."

"I am so happy, my dear friend. I promise God, and you, to be your faithful wife from this moment on until my death, and to proclaim this to my father, and to the priest who gives us the benediction of the Church, and to the whole world."

"I make the same pledge, my beloved, and I assure you that we are now perfectly married and belong to each other. Now come into my arms. We are going to seal our vows in bed."

"So soon? Is it possible that I could be so close to my happiness?"   (3: 263)

Although we may well laugh at this passage, the fact remains that Casanova does not change his mind after this night. He does not run away, and does indeed ask for C.C.'s hand in marriage through the mediation of M. de Bragadin, whom he has persuaded by his numerical calculations. C.C.'s father refuses to give him his daughter, however, and sends her off to a convent. Was Casanova assured of this refusal in advance? It is quite possible, since he had been forewarned of a refusal several times by C.C.'s brother and mother. Casanova had to obey social conventions in order to deflower this virgin, and he was astute enough to succeed in convincing himself that the marriage was possible. There is yet another clue to Casanova's self-deception; as early as his second night with C.C., from whom he has by now obtained everything, his flame is slightly dampened: "Uncertainty, fear, and deceptive hope made the pleasures of love much less intense during the last two hours that we spent together" (2: 275). Of course, he has already distanced himself—but he does not admit this, for that would be too dangerous. He is merely lovesick and still considers C.C. his wife. He nonetheless abandons any idea of rescuing the young girl from her convent: "I saw that such a rescue would be difficult, and because P.C. was in prison, I found that it would also be difficult to correspond with my wife—for I believed her to be my wife by a bond that was much stronger than any union that could have joined us before the Church and a notary" (2: 276). Hence Casanova is truly caught, as if the trap of deception he had set had closed on him. What extraordinary tale will he invent to get out of this fix?

He may not have changed very much, after all. He quite subtly arranges circumstances so that he will be relieved of the obligation to marry, not by his own doing, but by the vigilance of a father who wants to protect his daughter. Casanova bears no responsibility in the matter. Although he is guilty (since he has indeed seduced this girl), he is innocent because he was sincere in wanting to marry her. He cannot be blamed for the failure of their plans, particularly given that he considers himself married and repeats constantly that she is truly his wife. He may not have changed, but he is at least forced to make a concession. He has in fact known for several years that he cannot claim that the laws of marriage are meaningless, and that he can master the thunder and all forces that defy taboos. He knows, therefore, that he must create a state of blindness and illusion for his own sake and that, although he may find it easy to sleep with a woman when he is paying for it, it becomes impossible when love is involved. Casanova is decidedly not and could never be a Don Juan, for he has no sense of the tragic side of existence, never suspects the consequences of his actions, and certainly does not want to assume responsibility for them. But because he does not (and never will) have a statue of a commander, a father, or a true law to confront, he must adhere to custom, the soft underbelly of legality, and believe himself honest, moral, and generous. Thus his fear of women obliges him to respect them and do everything possible to leave them on good terms, so that they will never become his enemies—for then nothing would protect him from their violence.

One must admit that Casanova is supremely astute on this point. Rather than revolting against the law, he subverts it by exploiting those who uphold it. He succeeds in finding an ex-future-father-in-law who acts like a true father by imposing a veritable interdiction. This father is not Casanova's dupe, yet he allows him to avoid submitting to the law—and better yet, obliges him to ignore it. Hence Casanova surmounts still another limit: he manages to get a forbidding father to do exactly what is necessary to ensure Casanova's escape after Casanova has seduced the daughter—and so further undermines the father's law. Thus the interdiction imposed by C.C.'s father provides Casanova with an excellent occasion to dispense with any concern for the law.

We should not, however, reach our conclusions too quickly. This entire strategy is subtle, fragile even. If the refusal of C.C.'s father had resulted in liberating Casanova so completely that he forgot the woman he had come to consider his eternal wife, he would have lost all faith in the sincerity of his earlier promise. And then his whole defense system would have crumbled. To the contrary, if he is to be cured of his fear of women, Casanova must pass himself off as a faithful little husband for a while longer, in order to prove to himself that he did not seek out the paternal refusal—that he not only did not want or expect it, but had nothing to do with it—because it does not change his eternal sentiments in the least. Anyone else but Casanova would be taking a considerable risk of never getting out of this affair. But we can rest assured that his imagination and his fortune are quite healthy and functioning. He will invent a magnificent scenario for this occasion, one that is both perfectly suited to the magnitude of the situation and designed to rid him of his dear wife with no regrets or remorse.

We must backtrack a bit to get a hint of the scenario that he is now preparing for us. We recall that Casanova first meets Pier Capretta, C.C.'s brother, and his mistress, Mme C., as the victims of a road accident. This Capretta serves as a matchmaker: he does not settle for inviting Casanova to his home to meet C.C., but goes so far as to leave them the key to a *casin* (what we would call a studio apartment) where they can meet and make love. That is not all. One scene in particular reveals who this Capretta really is and also shows Casanova's still unadmitted intentions. After an evening at the opera, the two couples—Capretta and Mme C., Casanova and C.C.— go out to dinner together. At the end of the meal, Capretta "throws himself on a sofa, dragging Mme C., who had drunk too much, with him" (3: 257), and the two engage in a full exhibition. The still innocent C.C. turns her back on them, only to find herself facing a mirror, thanks to which she does not miss a single moment of the spectacle. Casanova maintains his reserve in this instance. It is nonetheless this libertine episode that will prove decisive in his relations with C.C. The next day, just as she is about to give herself to him, "she told me that she was sure we would not be bored, and having taken off her mask and her cloak, she threw herself into my arms and said that I had won her soul completely at that frightful supper where I had treated her so tactfully" (3: 261). C.C. is undoubtedly won over by the respect that Casanova showed her; but at the same time, she can wait no longer, for the sight of her brother and his mistress has heightened her desire. It is the very same scene that makes Casanova's love "invincible" (3: 259). He decides to marry C.C. in order to save her, as he puts it, from her brother's libertinage; he does not mention that it is precisely this libertinage that had fascinated him, and that he will shrewdly set into motion with C.C., through a series of complicated detours that, obviously, will not be his doing.

This anecdote is hardly negligible, for it prefigures what will become manifest in several chapters right up to the end of the third volume and for a good part of the fourth. This will take us from June 1753 to July 1755, when two new figures arrive on the scene: M.M., a nun who is a friend of C.C.'s, and Cardinal de Bernis, the French ambassador to Venice.

C.C. stays in secret contact with her lover during her stay in the convent. So that she may see him, Casanova regularly attends mass in the chapel of the convent where she is confined. One day, he receives a letter from a nun he calls M.M., whom historians have never been able to identify. She tells him that she had noticed him in church and proposes various ways to arrange a possible meeting. So begins a doubly complicated romantic intrigue. First of all, though the nun has some accomplices, she does not enjoy complete freedom of action; she can only sneak out of the convent at night and by gondola, for the convent is located in Murano. Furthermore, she has a high-placed lover, Cardinal de Bernis, who, far from frowning upon this adventure, proves to be its most cunning agent. As if all of this were not already complicated enough, we learn that, back at the convent, M.M. and C.C. have "a liaison that could not be more tender" (4: 85).

These chapters lay out before us the figures of a veritable carousel. The four figures will find themselves engaged in calculated jousting matches in which their respective positions will vary endlessly. After their first exchange of letters, Casanova and M.M. meet for the first time at Bernis's *casin* (4: 37). They have their second tryst in a *casin* that Casanova has rented (4: 48), where M.M. shows that she is a free thinker, liberated from religion. Their third meeting takes place in Bernis's *casin*. M.M. arrives this time in her religious habit (4: 57) and informs Casanova that Bernis had been present during their first evening together, hidden in a secret adjoining room where he could observe them without being seen (4: 60). She asks Casanova if he will agree to let Bernis watch their upcoming tryst in this manner, although Bernis will not know that Casanova knows. M.M. arrives "dressed like a sophisticated, worldly lady" (4: 64), and they stage a grand erotic scene inspired by the positions that Pietro Aretino immortalized. Casanova learns through a letter from C.C. that she is fully aware of the situation, and that M.M. is her intimate friend. M.M. sends C.C. to the *casin* in her place, but slips into Bernis's hiding place in the adjoining room, where she witnesses a long conversation between C.C. and Casanova, who is unable to touch his former "wife." Casanova, Bernis, and M.M. dine together soon afterward; M.M. suggests inviting C.C. to join them as a fourth dinner partner the next time (4: 111), whence follows a dinner for four, during which Bernis flirts with C.C. (4: 114). They plan to meet again (4: 117), but Bernis finds a pretext to be absent. So Casanova makes love with C.C. and M.M., who have both begun to show him all they know. There is yet another meeting planned for the foursome (4: 122); but this time it is Casanova who invents an excellent excuse not to come, which leads to a session of lovemaking by the trio Bernis, M.M., and C.C. The four meet one last time: Bernis sleeps with C.C., Casanova with M.M. The exchange has now been made, the circle is complete. Bernis will soon leave Venice, and Casanova and M.M. will little by little drift apart.

Casanova's most obvious aim throughout this story is to get out of his promise to marry C.C. After a series of detours that are as long as they are necessary, he attains his goal, the moment when C.C. is unfaithful to him by sleeping with Bernis. When he has C.C. and M.M. to himself, he wonders whether, in the upcoming tryst, he would cede his place to Bernis:

While caught in this unfortunate conflict between reason and prejudice, nature and sentiment, I could not decide whether to attend the supper or to forgo it. If I were to attend it, we would all spend the night obliged to maintain decency, and I would seem ridiculous, jealous, greedy, and impolite. If I were to forgo it, C.C. would be lost, at least to my mind. I sensed that I would no longer love her and would certainly have no further thought of marrying her. (4: 121)

Hence, during this episode, Casanova is on the verge of being relieved of the woman he had always wanted to consider his wife.

We should not, however, overlook the fact that this operation is no burden for him. Everything simply follows the order of events, and Félicien Marceau has insightfully demonstrated that it is not Casanova but M.M. who always plays the instigator.* To be more precise, it is Bernis who pulls the strings through M.M., who is completely in his thrall; it is Bernis who, out of his desire to have C.C., sees that Casanova would make excellent bait. Casanova himself realizes what kind of intrigue he has gotten into:

> I was sure that he had devised some scheme by which, despite all her loyalty, M.M. was to be the instigator; but she would carry out his plot with such skill and finesse that I would not see any evidence. Although I was not disposed to push my naturally accommodating spirit too far, I could nonetheless see that I would end up being the dupe of Bernis, and that C.C. would be stolen away from me.   (4: 116)

He later acknowledges that he had "to grin and bear it" (4: 122).

As the text reveals upon close examination, Bernis's strategy goes exactly as planned. We should not forget, however, that Casanova is particularly well suited to allowing someone else to be the instigator. It is essential for him that this whole business be beyond his responsibility from beginning to end. When, during a conversation in front of Bernis, M.M. casually mentioned that the foursome would eventually meet, Casanova had already been forced to approve the plan: "They had plotted together so that when the subject came up in conversation I would have to approve it myself out of politeness, sentiment, and fair play. The ambassador, whose position clearly entailed knowing how to carry out an intrigue most effectively, had succeeded in his plan, and I had walked right into it" (4: 113).

Likewise, when Bernis leaves him alone with C.C. and M.M., Casanova will see no other choice befitting good manners and fair play but to abstain in turn from attending the next tryst. He is manipulated like a child; but curiously, he can only invoke proper etiquette to argue in his defense. Although he is a mere plebeian dealing with a patrician's daughter and a French ambassador, Casanova does not neglect proper manners: "I felt sure that the ambassador's

---

* *Une Insolente Liberté: les aventures de Casanova* (Gallimard, 1983), pp. 134–39.

absence had been planned. They had predicted that I would suspect this and feel so grateful and honor bound that I would not want to be less courageous than they in trampling nature underfoot, out of an enlightened sentiment and a sense of obligation to be as generous and polite as they were" (4: 120–21).

Although it is indeed the ambassador who plans the intrigue and M.M. who carries it out, the episode nevertheless unfolds according to Casanova's strategy, a strategy that cannot make itself explicit without destroying itself. It is absolutely essential that our libertine appear to be the dupe of his accomplices and make us believe that he has been manipulated, for he could not be innocent if he were not irresponsible. He is surely not a voyeur like Bernis and M.M., but he is undeniably a spectator to this play—an uninvolved spectator: "I had no thought either of consenting to or opposing this. . . . This intrigue might have consequences that made me apprehensive, yet I was extremely curious to see how it would end" (4: 116).

The strategy of misprision is very difficult to handle, particularly when one is writing. With the slightest slip or twist of a sentence, Casanova and his reader might realize that he is quite actively involved in this story, and that he is as scheming as the others. It is therefore essential that even the most wary reader be taken in, that he be moved by the story of this poor man who is being hoaxed by a couple of aristocrats. Casanova must have chuckled from time to time at the trick he succeeded in playing on his "dear readers." Rives Childs, who has a soft spot for Casanova, yet watches and occasionally scolds him from his vantage point of disapproving historian, makes this remark: "So taken up was he with his own feelings, supreme egoist that he was, he never appreciated the undertones of his own recital.* And while discussing the correspondence between Casanova and Henriette (which has never reached us), the more cautious Marceau writes: "For lack of these letters, there are details to be gleaned from all of this that are all the more interesting in that Casanova was probably not aware of their import."†

I would not be so sure of that. One should always be wary with writers and their pressing need to lead the reader astray so that he

---

* *Casanova: A Biography*, p. 61.
† *Une Insolente Liberté*, p. 114.

will not hamper their efforts to write; and this particular writer strikes me as a certified master of the art of misleading. In any case, we can detect some of his most constant preoccupations among the details he randomly throws into his text, in the ballet he has his characters dance.

It is the liaison between C.C. and M.M. that makes possible the multiple configurations assumed by the foursome in this quadrille. There is more than a mere woman-to-woman relationship between C.C. and M.M. C.C. uses the formulas heard earlier from Nanette and Marton to explain the nature of her relationship to M.M.: "You know full well that she loves me, and that I am often her wife and her little husband; and as you find nothing wrong in my being your rival, she does not want you to think that her love is akin to hate either" (4: 88). Hence not only are gender roles reversible between these two women, but C.C. has the same gender as Casanova, since she is his rival and makes M.M. happy. A bit later, she says, "It does not anger us that you love us both. Did I not write to you saying that I wished I could cede you my place?" (4: 89). By taking the place of C.C. here, Casanova becomes a woman just like her. When the same C.C. speaks of Bernis, she identifies with him in becoming M.M.'s husband: "Even if I loved him, I would not necessarily go and tell him that. And besides, I am sure that he loves my wife" (4: 118). M.M. makes the same passage from one sexual role to another, by including an intermediate role that is devoid of sex: she presents herself successively as a man (4: 49), a nun (4: 57), and a lady (4: 64). And to make the merry-go-round spin at its top speed, M.M. fills in for Bernis in the secret hiding place, and Bernis takes Casanova's place in relation to the two women, who can thereby exchange their men. It is no surprise that the climax of Casanova's night with C.C. and M.M. is reached in a state of complete gender confusion: "All three of us were so intoxicated by voluptuousness, so incited by all hindrances to the satisfaction of our desires and carried away by our continual furies, that we wreaked havoc upon everything visible and palpable that nature had provided; we devoured all within sight as we pleased, and found that all three of us became the same sex in each trio we performed" (4: 120).

"All three of us became the same sex"—but which one? Precisely, neither: their devastation and devouring manifest a desire to be omnipotent, a desire that undermines the very principle of gender difference. The exchange and constant circulation of partners would be meaningless for Casanova if it did not lead to this indistinction, which makes him the true master.

If we reduce the succession of relations among the four participants to its simplest expression, we are left with the following schema:

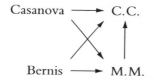

Casanova ⟶ C.C.

Bernis ⟶ M.M.

The two women have therefore had sexual relations with the two men and with each other. But the two men have only had sex with the two women. If the quadrille were to be truly complete, Casanova would have had to have intercourse with Bernis. However, if this had been the case, if such a solution had been possible for Casanova, then the complicated scenario would not have been necessary. The intrigue is intended precisely to preserve a distance between the two men, even while showing quite distinctly, through this missing link, that the distance is abolished—that is, that the tie between the men is the key that explains the whole adventure.

After all, Casanova could have recounted a truly four-sided intrigue. He is not, in any case, absolutely opposed to homosexuality. We saw him engage in it with Ismail in Constantinople, and there are other traces of it in the *Memoirs*. He is not, however, the kind of man who would content himself very long with such a short circuit in order to resolve the question he must confront in his relation to women. His brand of homosexuality passes most often through women; Casanova always entrusts them with the task of establishing communication between men.

Yet the question raised here is perhaps not a question of homosexuality, or for that matter of heterosexuality. Rather, it is a question of discreetly affirming infantile omnipotence, by confusing gender, if possible, or else by circulating women between men. The magician who believes that he can dig up hidden treasures may not be very far removed from all of this. He can be found somewhere between the swindler who always finds a hen that lays golden eggs and the ambassador who serves the man who possesses all women. These two figures are indeed akin to Casanova, characters with whom he willingly identifies when he takes or gives them women.

The swindler, in this case, is none other than Pier Capretta who, as we know, is highly adept at passing bills of exchange; he is inscribed in a long lineage of impostors of all kinds: shysters who fill their pockets at will like magic fairies, or alchemists, such as Saint-Germain, who promise to produce precious stones for the king. We have seen the telling parallel established between the couple formed by Capretta and his mistress, and that formed by Casanova and C.C. The author of the *Memoirs* takes great pains to remind us of Capretta's existence when he describes the first dinner shared by the present foursome. The allusion is incongruous here, for the author is forced to slip it into this passage as a way of interpreting a smile from C.C. that could actually mean anything, and more probably nothing at all other than contentment: "She looked at me with a smile on her lips, and I understood perfectly the language her soul was speaking: she wanted to draw my attention to the difference between this gathering and the evening the year before when her brother had given her such a rude exhibition of worldliness (4: 111).

The second figure, that of the king who has limitless power in his dealings with women, first appears a few pages earlier, during Casanova's initial encounter with Bernis. Casanova recounts an anecdote; we may well ask why he chooses this one in particular, if not to suggest that he has accepted the idea of adding C.C. to the trio that he has formed with M.M. and Bernis:

> It was then that I told him the story of O'Morphi [Morfi] in all of its details. This narration pleased him immensely. He begged me to show him her portrait. He told me that she was still in the Parc-aux-Cerfs, where she gave the king great delight, and had borne him a child. They left quite content at eight o'clock, and I remained in the *casin*.

The following morning, since I had given my word to M.M., I wrote to C.C. without forewarning her that someone she had never met would be joining our party.   (4: 111)

Just as Casanova had become the king somewhat by transferring Morfi from his arms to those of Louis XV, so C.C. will serve as a link between Bernis—the king's envoy in this circumstance—and the Venetian. And just in case we haven't yet grasped the significance of the comparison, our memoirist gives us a second chance. On the same page, he concludes a note addressed to M.M. with the following description of Bernis: "Your friend is the king of all men" (4: 111). He said it quite clearly: not just the king of France, the king of all men. And I, Casanova, give him my woman.

The Most Powerful of Men

It is January 1755 when Bernis leaves Venice. Casanova continues to see M.M., but his enthusiasm is waning. For the moment at least, thanks to his participation in the quadrille, he is freed from his terrible fear and can "pick the lovely flower" of Tonine (4: 152–53) and, shortly thereafter, of her sister Barberine (4: 178–81), both of whom are his serving girls. He does not stop when he is on such a lucky roll. While lodging with a family that includes several daughters, he learns that the oldest girl is ailing, and that because she isn't having her monthly "benefits," she must be bled regularly to keep from suffocating. Her physician is convinced that "the true remedy to cure her would be a robust lover" (4: 182). The ever-generous Casanova offers to be the apothecary: "We spent the entire night together; I was animated by love and the desire to cure her, and she by gratitude and the most extraordinary voluptuousness. . . . She slept with me three weeks in a row without interruption and never had any trouble breathing, and her 'benefits' returned" (4: 191). We have already seen Casanova serving as a physician of this ilk when he undertook to cure the pretty newlywed of her fear of lightning. And we shall see him use the same technique in attempting to bring on an abortion. Hence long before certain figures who pride themselves on making the discovery, Casanova found the instrument of universal medicine. The sorcerer must, after all, be a healer as well.

All of these successes do not prevent the clouds that hover over his head from lingering there. There are spies commissioned by the state inquisitors on his tail. His friends, M. de Bragadin in particular, advise him to leave. Casanova does nothing of the sort: "To conclude my argument, I told him that I would declare myself guilty if I were to leave, for an innocent who could have no reason for remorse would have no further cause for fear" (4: 199). The next day, July 26, 1755—he has just turned thirty—Casanova is arrested and sent to the Leads (the roof of this terrible Venetian prison was lead-covered, whence its name). He had refused to run away in order to show, as he says, that he was free of remorse and therefore innocent; but remaining in Venice was also a way of paying the price for his self-avowed offense, so that he would never owe anything more to anyone. He enumerates a long list of charges made against him—magician, atheist, disturber of the peace, breaker of Lent every day, accomplice to foreign ministers—and he knows that there is not one of these charges of which he would not be found guilty if he were scrutinized by a diligent tribunal, and this one is excellent. In the *Précis de ma vie*, written a year before his death, he remarks: "The state inquisitors of Venice had me confined to the Leads for fair and sensible reasons."* One could say that he needs periodically to descend into hell, to sink once again into horror and sordidness. This is not the first time that we see him preparing the path to failure even at the height of success, and hence letting himself be crushed by the machine that he himself has set into place and motion. This is perhaps a necessary step back into reality, a step facilitated by the brutality of a society that seeks to avenge itself against someone who has tried to realize his phantasms.

Hence he has just passed from the highest to the lowest, from the greatest of liberties to the strictest imprisonment, for none of his friends can do anything more for him. But the pendulum is not slow in swinging back. After spending over a year in the Leads, our champion of evasion escapes from his guards, a feat that no one before him had managed to do. This extraordinary escape makes him a unique man not only in Venice, but in all of Europe. The tale

---

**Mémoires (Bibliothèque de la Pléiade, Gallimard, 1964), 2: 1140.

that he goes on to tell of his escape (which takes two hours to re-count; 5: 20) will act as a talisman for him, piquing the public's curiosity and winning its admiration, and, finally, opening many doors to him. His account of this adventure, written on Bernis's request, will be the only portion of the *Memoirs* published during the author's lifetime.

This unique (as he shall clearly demonstrate) man flees Venice and passes through Germany to arrive in Paris on January 5, 1757, the day of Damien's foiled attempt to assassinate Louis XV. If historians had not confirmed this date, we might think that Casanova in-vented it, so well does it fit this volume—which Casanova was al-ready preparing during the account of his adventures with his friend Bernis, "the king of all men" (4: 111). Once again, however, the pendulum will swing in the opposite direction. Casanova, who leaves the Leads in utter misery, will lead an extravagant life for two years and end up ruined, forced to leave Paris in the midst of catas-trophe, after having been incarcerated in For-l'Evêque (5: 256). This volume could just as easily be entitled *I am the King* as *From One Prison to the Other* or *From One Escape to Another*.

As soon as he arrives in the capital, Casanova rushes to see Ber-nis, who has just been named minister of state. Bernis introduces his old friend to Choiseul and M. de Boulogne, the general con-troller; and he presents him to them as "a financial wizard" (5: 21). These gentlemen need 20,000,000 francs for the Ecole Militaire founded by Mme de Pompadour, which took in children at the time. Casanova barely keeps from bursting out laughing when he hears of the qualities with which Bernis has endowed him. A few days later, Bernis himself tells Casanova that "he would wager that, without him, I would never have noticed that I had such an exten-sive knowledge of finances" (5: 29). Far from blowing his cover, Casanova joins in the game and, without giving himself away, sug-gests a vague project about which he hasn't the foggiest idea. M. du Vernai, who is in charge of funding the Ecole Militaire, is in-trigued and summons Casanova once more. We get a marvelous view of our adventurer's technique in this episode. He has, first of all, an amazing ability to conform to the expectations of his audi-ence: since everyone is convinced that he is a financial wizard, he becomes one on the spot. Second, he is one of the sliest of all magicians, for he knows how to discover what other people are thinking by making them formulate it. No one can surpass him in this area: "If he thinks he can worm information out of me, I dare him to try it; when he tells me his [plan], it will be up to me to say whether he guessed [mine] or not, and, if I can grasp what he is talking about, I will perhaps say something more; if I do not understand a thing, I will remain mysteriously silent" (5: 22).

That is exactly what happens. The next time Casanova sees M. du Vernai, the minister gives him a folio notebook and tells him, "Here is your project" (5: 23). The notebook contains a proposition for a lottery, a project that the Calsabigi brothers (one of whom is a mathematician) are trying to get accepted by the authorities. Casanova replies without hesitation that this is indeed what he had in mind. And he immediately contacts the Calsabigi to learn what this is all about, without ever letting them suspect his ignorance. His experience as a gambler has already provided some opportunity for dabbling in probability calculations. Casanova deals briskly with this affair, and his loquaciousness and newly acquired expertise work wonders in stifling all possible objections. In a few weeks, Casanova procures what the Calsabigi brothers had failed to obtain after two years of negotiations, thanks to his hotheadedness, savvy, luck, and, of course, the protection of Bernis and Mme de Pompadour. The official authorizations are granted; Casanova is given six lottery offices and a stipend. He sells five of these offices and keeps one, where he pays off the winning tickets—not eight days after the drawing, as had been planned, but the next day. Everyone flocks to his office. He becomes rich and assured of a regular income.

Casanova is amazingly quick to attain new knowledge, because he is no less amazingly adept at identifying with another person. He is able to talk and intoxicate himself with his own occasionally invented stories precisely because he knows how to listen and, more important, make someone else talk, so that he can assimilate the other's thoughts. His own discourse is a reply, a reaction to what he hears that is called up from the depths of his being; for however shallow he seems, he allows what he hears to go right through and permeate him. Yet even when "possessed" by his interlocutor, he is able to pull back, recover his lucidity, and detect the weak spot that will allow him to manipulate the other. He is all the more adept at detecting this for having given himself over altogether for a moment. He is a formidable, perfectly disguised wolf who has worked his way into the flock of sheep. Thanks to his pure sincerity, he breaks down the resistance of his interlocutor; and then his ruse takes control. In this sense, no one is more credulous than he, for he panics at the idea that someone might not like him. Hence he believes in his interlocutor with all his heart; yet because nothing so repels him as to be had, no one is more sly in undoing his attachments and using them to trap whoever sought to make a fool of him. These are doubtless the secret weapons of Casanova as seducer and magician alike. There is nonetheless an element of Casanova the impostor present as well: as he demonstrates, with a bit of practice one can detach gullibility and even sincerity from the emotion that produced them, and turn them into cold-blooded weapons.

It is not surprising that, after the episode of the lottery, Casanova recounts his escapades with Count Tireta, an unparalleled cheater and womanizer who has arrived from Venice with Mme Manzoni's recommendations. This Tireta is twenty-five years old and devoted exclusively to gambling and women. Casanova advises him to find a wealthy old lady whom he could serve in his fashion, for Tireta seems well suited for such an arrangement. Tireta does indeed soon latch onto a woman named Lamberti, who nicknames him Six-coups; he later takes up with a Mme XXX. One day, while Tireta is attending to this lady, Casanova approaches one of Mme XXX's nieces, whom he calls Mlle de la M—re. He "casts his spell on her" by showing her his penis and ejaculating right in front of her during an evening salon gathering. He enjoys her ultimate favors, but not before learning that she is going to marry a merchant from Dunkirk a few weeks later. Casanova is as careful as ever to free himself of this woman before conquering her, even though he promises to marry her (but does nothing to stop her from wedding someone else).

The distinguishing marks of Casanova's brief period of connivance with Tireta are worth noting. Like so many of the adventures described in the *Memoirs*, the young count functions as Casanova's momentary double. Casanova uses this double to prepare himself and the reader for his efforts to dupe another old, wealthy woman. Tireta's pattern of living off of women who are well past their prime foreshadows Casanova's upcoming liaison with Mme d'Urfé. The promises of "Six-coups" and the audacity of our brazen hero are no doubt meant to be declarations of their irresistible sexual virility, but they actually sound more like the boasts of insecure adolescents or the bawdy tales of dirty old men. Casanova will later repeat the rather perfunctory method of seduction used with Mlle de la M—re, but at that point, it will be no more than a harbinger of impotence.

There is only one other adventure mentioned in this entire volume; it concerns a young, still-virginal bride and takes place a few weeks before Casanova's departure from Paris. Hence, between the beginning and the end of his two-year stay, "his love life [is] apparently uneventful" as Félicien Marceau puts it.* Casanova will not get anywhere with Esther, whom he meets in Holland; and he refrains from getting involved again with Thérèse Imer, whom he meets again during the same mission. As for Manon Balletti, who reappears periodically throughout this volume—and who had loved Casanova with intensity and freshness, but also with reserve (since she expected him to marry her)—Casanova seems both constant and hopeless in his sentiments for her: "The friendship and esteem that I felt for her family drove any idea of seduction out of my mind; but because I was growing more enamored of her each day, and could not think of asking for her hand in marriage, I had no idea what I could have been after" (5: 81). It is as if something were frozen in his dealings with women. The fact that he is now well past the age of thirty is undoubtedly starting to figure in the balance of his love life. That, however, does not suffice to explain this situation, so we shall have to look for another explanation.

Casanova has not, in any case, grown timid. Bernis comes up with the idea of enlisting Casanova for secret missions. He is soon sent off to Dunkirk to gather all pertinent information on the navy there. It would be simply unbearable if our hero were not suited to being a spy. Fortunately he does not let us down and carries out his mission quite handily. What is intriguing is the disequilibrium that one notices upon reading the tale of this journey. Whereas only a

---

* *Une Insolente Liberté: les aventures de Casanova* (Gallimard, 1983), p. 167.

few pages are devoted to the mission proper (5: 79–84), ten pages are taken up with the account of his tumultuous return to Paris. Bernis and Laville, his "consultant," had urged Casanova to be prudent and discreet, explaining that, should he get into difficulty, he could not count on them and would instead be disclaimed: "The only spies anyone avows are ambassadors" (5: 82). But Casanova forgets all of this advice. He arrives in Aire at night and finds the doors shut because of the war. He gets himself let in by claiming to be a courier. When the authorities learn that he is nobody's courier, they force him to spend the night with the guards. The next day, he has an altercation with the local commandant, who pretends to take him outside for a duel but then invites him to dine with a large company. Casanova admits that he was wrong. "But," he adds, "I was determined to play the VIP, and I felt obliged to continue playing that role" (5: 86). Things turn sour in Amiens, where customs officials wake him to ask whether he has anything to declare; he hurls insults at them as an answer. In retaliation, they painstakingly search his luggage and discover a bit of tobacco, which is considered contraband. He is ordered as a result to pay a heavy fine. He incites the local villagers, who turn against him, and then bursts in upon a half-finished luncheon attended by the quartermaster in charge of customs. The quartermaster agrees that the fine must be levied and refuses to back down. Things would have gotten ugly if not for the intervention of a military commissioner who knows "the fiery nature of Italians" (5: 94). Whereas the local commandant in Aire had immediately suspected that he was dealing with a genial con man, the quartermaster of Amiens forces Casanova to play his role to the hilt:

If Catalan laws ordain that I must pay 1,200 francs for seven ounces of tobacco that I possess for my personal use, I deny them and declare that I will not pay a penny. I will stay here, and send a courier to my ambassador, who will protest to the king that you have violated the rights of everyone in the Ile-de-France by persecuting me, and I will be vindicated. Louis XV is great enough not to want to have anything to do with this odd kind of assassination. In any case, if I am refused a reparation, this incident will become a major affair of state, for rather than putting to death all Frenchmen traveling in its provinces, my republic will respond by banishing them. Here is proof of who I am. Read. (5: 92)

This aging adolescent is certainly not lacking in self-confidence. To declare that his republic will take reprisal measures (when he is in fact a fugitive ignored by all Venetians in Paris), to claim to be the center of an affair of state (when his adversaries are merely observing rules in reaction to his insults), to be assured of the king's protection (while he is actually on a secret mission)—all of this hints that Casanova is slightly deranged here. Yet upon hearing such a speech, one not only wants to laugh, one also starts to wonder whether the hothead who pronounced it might really be important after all. But who does this upstart Venetian take himself for? Why, for nothing less than the equal of the dukes and dignitaries of France with whom he keeps company; for the cherished friend of Mme de Pompadour, who had spoken to him once or twice; for the unique man who astonished all the embassies with his escape from the Leads—in a word, for an extraordinary individual. This fellow is as puffed up as a frog trying to make himself as big as a bull.

It would be too much to ask a fellow living with such a delusion of grandeur to take any interest in women. As he writes, "During this journey, philandering and frivolity held no attraction for me; my mission was the sole object of my attention and of all my actions" (5: 84). He drives his point home by saying that he had met Mlle de la M—re, now Mme P., in Dunkirk and was astonished by his own coolness toward her: "I knew myself too well to attribute my behavior to virtue. So why did I act this way? An Italian proverb that serves to interpret nature reveals the true reason: 'C . . . no vuol pensieri'" (5: 84).* We can interpret this as indicating either that he is thinking a bit too much during this period to allow his reflexes to function normally, or that his thoughts have taken on disturbing proportions.†

Il cazzo non vuol pensieri: literally, "The penis wants no thoughts."

† J. Rives Childs has shown that the trip to Dunkirk actually preceded Casanova's involvement in the lottery; *Casanova: A Biography Based on New Documents* (London: Allen and Unwin, 1961), p. 93. This is quite feasible, given that Bernis surely had to test Casanova as a spy before appointing him financial expert. The literary context, however, required that Casanova's stay in Paris start off with something spectacular, namely the lottery. Casanova's escapades during his journey to Dunkirk can therefore be read not as mere caprices and mistakes, but as the reaction of the great man he believes himself to be. It never occurs to Rives Childs that Casanova might have *composed* his *Memoirs*.

Casanova has by now told us enough to make us ready to hear the tale of his extravagances with Mme d'Urfé. But not quite: he first needs to have Count de La Tour d'Auvergne introduce him to his aunt. Casanova takes advantage of this occasion to relate an anecdote that shows him in a particularly ridiculous light. One night he gets into a carriage with La Tour d'Auvergne and his mistress. Thinking he is taking the mistress's hand, Casanova covers it with kisses and begins to go a bit too far, when suddenly La Tour d'Auvergne says to him: "My dear friend, I do indeed appreciate a polite gesture, obviously native to your country, which I no longer believed I deserved; I hope that you did not accord it to me by mistake" (5: 99). The young count bursts out laughing and does not hesitate to spread the story, which gives Casanova a great reputation. For someone who specializes in confusing identity and gender, the adventure is perfect—not to mention the homosexual side of a friendship that is reinforced by a harmless duel (5: 102) and a cure achieved by applying a magic potion to La Tour's thigh (5: 104).

Mme d'Urfé is curious to meet a man who had already established a reputation as a magician during an earlier stay in Paris. She herself is quite well read in alchemy and chemistry, two fields that (like so many people during this period) she cannot distinguish. According to the specialists consulted by Rives Childs, she was "a researcher ahead of her time who possessed an extensive knowledge of her subject, and whose experiments should not be overlooked by a historian of science."* She is equally well acquainted with cabalistic literature. She is also, however, frightfully gullible, and Casanova will learn how to exploit this gullibility for seven years, and so win both her money and protection.

They talk for hours on end and are mutually bedazzled by each other's knowledge of all kinds of magic. Casanova begins cheating right away, at times pretending that he is the expert when he is actually guessing from details provided by the marquise. One day, she gives him a manuscript written in ciphers; and since he is unmatched in the art of deciphering, he easily discovers the key, a

---

*This observation was added to the second edition of the French translation of J. Rives Childs's biography: *Casanova*, tr. Francis-L. Mars, 2d ed. (Garnier Frères, 1983), p. 138.

magic word that Mme d'Urfé had thought she alone knew, "which she kept in her memory and had never written down." Casanova goes on:

> I could have told her the truth, that the very calculation I had used to decipher the manuscript had given away the magic word, but on a whim I told her that a genie had revealed it to me. It was by this false confession that I got Mme d'Urfé under my power. That day I made myself the arbitrator of her soul, and I abused my power. . . . Mme d'Urfé's great illusion was believing it possible to call up the so-called elementary spirits. She would have given everything she owned to achieve this; and she had known several impostors who had fooled her by pretending to teach her how. When she found herself with me, who had given her such clear evidence of my erudition, she believed that she had reached her goal. (5: 116)

Hence everything seems to be in place, for the impostor will be able to exploit Mme d'Urfé's conviction that he is the sole person capable of accomplishing this grand operation. In my opinion, however, that is only one side of this extraordinary conversation. Casanova thinks that only she is the victim of gullibility, and that he himself is absolutely immune from it; but the situation is not so simple. He could not have pulled off this hoax for so long were he not caught himself in a veritable delirium upheld by his partner; after all, as he learned in the episode of the knife and its sheath, he is eminently susceptible to just such a delirium. With Javotte, he had to play magician all by himself. In this case, it is Mme d'Urfé who inspires or awakens in him the kind of madness that is the most irrational yet perhaps most prevalent among human beings. She will come to consider him, to make him become, *His Majesty the Baby*. In a word, Mme d'Urfé's gullibility, which he has managed to tap, endows him with the omnipotence that every child is sure he possesses, a conviction that the vicissitudes of existence and age can only temper. It would be unthinkable not to quote this decisive page in its entirety:

> In her opinion, I possessed not only the philosopher's stone, but also the means to commune with all the elementary spirits. She consequently believed that I was capable of turning the whole world upside down, of determining the good or bad fortune of France, and therefore attributed my need to stay hidden to a perfectly understandable fear of being arrested and

imprisoned; for that would inevitably occur, in her view, should the minister ever become truly acquainted with me. These extravagances stemmed from the revelations her genie made to her during the night, which her over-fanciful imagination convinced her were real. In perfect good faith she told me one day that her genie had persuaded her that, because she was a woman, I could not initiate her into communion with the genies, but that, by means of an operation that I undoubtedly knew, I could transport her soul into the body of a male child born out of the philosophical coupling of an immortal male and a mortal woman, or of a mortal male with a divine female being.

I did not think that I was guilty of deception in encouraging this lady's crazy ideas, for she was utterly convinced, and I could not possibly succeed in disabusing her. If like a true honest man [*honnête homme*] I had told her that all her ideas were absurd, she would not have believed me; so I decided to go along with her. I could not help being pleased at being taken for the greatest of all the Rosicrucians and the most powerful of all men, by a lady related to the first families of France, and who, above all, had wealth that far surpassed the 80,000-pound income she gained from her land and her houses in Paris. I saw clearly that, if need be, she would not refuse me anything, and although I had devised no scheme for profiting from her riches, in whole or in part, I nonetheless could not bear the thought of renouncing this power. (5: 119–20)

Hence the sentence "She consequently believed that I was capable of turning the whole world upside down, of determining the good or bad fortune of France" is juxtaposed to "I could not help being pleased at being taken for the greatest of all the Rosicrucians and the most powerful of all men." Casanova's dream of omnipotence is undoubtedly intertwined here with a full awareness of the fraud he is perpetrating. I tend to think, however, that Casanova's hoax would not have been possible if Mme d'Urfé had not reactivated the dream that lies at the very heart of his personality. The unique man to take on a powerful state, friend to Bernis (the "king of all men"), the man who, lacking any means or knowledge, nonetheless fills the king's treasury with gold, who arouses the pity of His Serene Highness—this man is closely akin to the little boy who was revived by the witch; and all the personas that make up the man Casanova find it quite normal that Fortune should shower its favors on him (5: 11). I wonder, in fact, whether fraud in general does not stem from an unshakable belief in the omnipotence felt during childhood. We are occasionally astonished to see sensible people get involved in such obviously risky, implausible schemes. They do so because they believe in the protection provided by their magic genie, whatever actions they may undertake. Not just anyone can be an impostor; one needs a healthy dose of infantile certitude, still fresh. Casanova needs to be an impostor—that is, to see money flow in great streams through his fingers, women fall at his feet, happenstance pull him out of the worst fixes—because he believes in his omnipotence. Of course, he recognizes his bad faith and his illicit methods; if he did not, he would quite simply be a madman who would have to be shut away in an asylum. In this long passage, however, we can see that he situates himself alternately on two levels: the level of omnipotence, a quality in which he cannot help believing, since this great lady furnishes the conviction and the signs; and the level of fraud, which emerges in his moments of lucidity and skepticism. And his lucidity and disbelief can in turn reinforce his sense of omnipotence, because this infantile conviction knows itself, as only a god could.

What does Mme d'Urfé think Casanova capable of? The question is not without significance, given what we know about him. The drama of the marquise lies in her regret over being a woman, for only men can accede to communion with the elementary spirits (the spirits of the four elements). She wants her soul to pass into a male child—that is, she seeks a passage from one sex to another, a substitution of identity and gender. When one knows the lengths to which Casanova has gone in his romantic endeavors to effect this kind of substitution, one can guess how forcefully the words of the marquise resonate in him. She offered to bring about once and for all the long-sought passage from one gender to another that he could achieve only in rare instances. Félicien Marceau notes in passing this characteristic trait: "This theme of substitution—which culminates in the suppression of identity and is, in the end, the theme of indifference or non-difference—is also the principle underlying certain forms of orgy."* When one hears this from a reader who is so attentive to the text yet so little inclined to indulge in venturesome interpretations of this sort, one must conclude that,

* *Une Insolente Liberté*, p. 173.

through sheer repetition, the *Memoirs* have accustomed him to such a vision.

Could we not, however, go a bit further? Is there not an intrinsic tie between infantile omnipotence and the abolition of differences of gender and identity? One can answer the question simply by posing it. As soon as one establishes a difference—and the differences in question are fundamental—one enters the realm of the relative. In Casanova's dispersed world, the omnipotence he seeks functions just like his strategy of substitution, reducing diversity (of women) to an appearance of unvaried sameness. The faster one element changes into another, the greater will be the impression of continuity, of permanence, be it orderly or disorderly. Whence Casanova's indefatigable traveling from one place to another, from one undertaking to a new one, from one woman to the next. To maintain the phantasm of omnipotence, one must accelerate displacement, so that temporality can be reduced to an instant. For the seducer—that is, the seducer multiplied and viewed at the very heart of his seduction—there are only instants, indeed only a single instant, for the last instant is always the newest, the most primary. Inasmuch as he wants to be the agent of omnipotence, the seducer, or the adventurer, must have at his disposal a uniform, indistinct world with which he can do anything and everything—that is, nothing, for omnipotence should not have to be exercised. Generalized substitution is merely a weak alibi for reestablishing the world in the primitive, undifferentiated state it should never have lost.

Given that, at this moment of his existence—when caught up in a madness shared with Mme d'Urfé—Casanova seems to be completely possessed by this phantasm, one can see why his love life is consequently reduced to nothing, and why he can no longer fathom "what I could have been after" (5: 81) with Manon Balletti, as with women in general. It is as if he has become entangled in a sort of confusion in which successive and distinct romantic undertakings no longer make any sense for him. In his belief that he can do anything, he feels the same confusion he had felt at the time of his passage through horror and of his stay in the Leads, when he just barely missed losing his head. His power over distinct women is diminished in like measure, for he has set out to mix gender and identities until they are inextricable. What interests him in Amsterdam is not Esther, a particular woman, but rather the opportunity to bedazzle her and her father, Thomas Hope (a Freemason, like Casanova), with his cabala, and to persuade them that he can guess everything at a distance, without looking. Nor does he waste any time with Thérèse Imer, who would surely welcome his advances; he is interested only in her son (and in her daughter, but that is another story to which we shall return), for he would like to use the boy as the male child needed to bring about the regeneration of Mme d'Urfé. With Miss XCV, he can make love only by becoming a magician—that is, he follows Mme d'Urfé's counsel on how to use Arophe (5: 194), the philosopher's scent, and offers himself as a syringe to inject this substance into Miss XCV in order to induce an abortion. In contrast, when he sets out to build himself a harem—after the fashion of Louis XV's Parc-aux-Cerfs, as Rives Childs suggests*—it will signal the beginning of the end, for power over all women is merely a pale reflection of omnipotence. And when he does have a new love affair (with Mme Baret, the young bride), this exception will serve to mark the end of this period; it also concludes the last chapter of the volume. Once he has descended again into reality, he will have no recourse but to flee.

Casanova: A Biography, p. 109.

The End of the First Act

The story of Casanova and Mme d'Urfé is not over yet. According-ing to her reading of cabalistic literature, no woman can have the privilege of communing with the elementary spirits, which has been her lifelong dream. She is convinced that her friend holds the power to "transport her soul into the body of a male child" (5: 119), and she is ready to die for that, for she is sure that she will be reborn immediately afterward; she even has on hand a special poison nec-essary to carry this out. Casanova is more than mildly worried by such determination, but if he is to stay in the marquise's good graces, he must find some way to continue to kindle her enthusi-asm for "the big operation." For the moment, the operation can-not be performed, because at the end of September 1759, he is sent to Holland on another secret mission. Whereas his first mission, carried out in 1758 and entailing some difficult financial negotia-tions, had been a success befitting the delusions of grandeur he had at the time, the second is a failure: he cannot obtain a loan sought by the French government. It may well be that this mission is more arduous, but the most important reason for its failure is that the envoy is no longer in the same frame of mind. His arrest, his run-ins with the police, his departure amid suspicion, have all taken a toll on his sense of omnipotence. There is an unmistakable sign of this: after his arrival in Amsterdam, Esther, whom he had initiated into the cabala during his earlier visit, tells him that she is sure "his

answers come out of his own head" (6: 6). He succeeds once more
in fooling her, and persuades her that he is not the author of his
oracles by insisting that it is a genie who speaks through him. Soon
afterward, however, in an astonishingly dramatic turn of events, he
cannot keep from unmasking himself and explaining to Esther how
he had gone about fooling her (6: 39). He concludes this episode in
the following manner:

> I returned quite content to my inn, feeling as if I had been relieved of a heavy
> burden. The next day I brought her all the books I could find, which could
> not fail to amuse her. There were good and bad books among them, but I
> had warned her of this. My conics [*Conics*, by the Greek author Apollonius
> Pergaeus] pleased her because she found it truthful. If she was to be as out-
> standing as she wished in giving oracles, she would have to become a good
> physicist, and I steered her onto the right path. I thereafter decided to go
> on a brief journey to Germany before returning to Paris.   (6: 39–40)

Casanova has definitely turned over a new leaf. From this point
on he will no longer use the cabala, and his extravagances with
Mme d'Urfé will not resound as they did before; they will become
simply the tricks of a con man who has lost the sense of omnipotence that this woman had awakened in him. It is as if the scales had
fallen from his eyes: he sees that he can no longer rival Louis XV,
that he will no longer be the magical supplier of the royal treasury
(since he has just failed in that area), that someone who is as attracted to lowly dives as he cannot rub shoulders with the high and
mighty. His power of imagination has been snuffed out. In fact, it
is not insignificant that, as he confides to Esther, his decision to
leave for Germany seems to stem directly from the vanishing of his
magic secrets; for rich as this journey is in sleazy brawls, romantic
encounters, magnificent celebrations, threats of imprisonment, and
escapes, it offers no further opportunity for him to stage any new
scenarios in which his phantasms could be deployed. We hear the
same old refrain: women enjoyed in haste; others seduced by promises of marriage, whom he then hurries to marry off; substitutions
of identities; nuns and lesbians. The panoply is complete, but he
has already shown it to us so many times!

By his move away from the cabala and magic, he comes to consider differently the influence of fatality over his life, which he had

always defined according to the *Sequere Deum* he frequently invoked after first hearing it from Malipiero (1: 117). He had already given the reader a preview of this change after his first triumphant visit to Holland and before his return to Paris, where his troubles were to start: "*Destiny* is a meaningless word; it is we who make our destiny, despite the Stoics' axiom *Volentem ducit, nolentem trahit.** I am too self-indulgent when I apply it to myself" (5: 165). The same theme will reappear consistently hereafter, over the course of the years to follow (5: 181; 6: 23, 87; 7: 176; etc.). The fact that he can no longer "look at himself as a machine" (7: 176) changes his life in many respects. When his sense of omniscience, which he had sought to uphold with various forms of magic, fades away before his eyes, it is his innocence—so subtly protected—that is snuffed out. This modified vision of himself transforms him into a Venetian who grows less and less lighthearted.

After Germany, he travels to Switzerland, and then to Italy through the south of France, and subsequently returns to Germany, ending up in Paris during the last days of 1761. Mme d'Urfé has set up an apartment where he devotes himself entirely to preparations for the big operation by which she is to be reborn as a man.† This is how the operation is supposed to be carried out:

> In a location to be disclosed through inspiration from the genies, I was to find a virgin, the daughter of another disciple [of the cabala], and I was to impregnate her with a boy using a technique known only by brother Rosicrucians. This son was to be born alive, but with nothing but a sensitive soul. Mme d'Urfé was to take the child into her arms at the moment of birth and keep him next to her in her own bed for seven days. At the end of these seven days, she would die while pressing her lips to those of the infant, who would thereby receive her intelligent soul.
>
> After this permutation, I was to care for the child with all of my customary dignity; and as soon as the child reached the age of three, Mme d'Urfé would recognize herself [would be reborn], and then I would begin to initiate her into complete knowledge of this great science.   (8: 39–40)

***Ducunt volentem fata, nolentem trahunt*: "Fate leads the willing, drags the unwilling."

†We have nothing but Laforgue's censored version of the first four chapters of volume 8. Laforgue did not return this part of the manuscript to Brockhaus; hence it appears to be lost forever.

Casanova furnishes the so-called virgin by summoning a Mlle Corticelli from Prague—a fifteen-year-old dancer whom he had known in Florence. Mme d'Urfé awaits them in her chateau at Pontcarré and welcomes them with all the pomp imaginable. That evening, Casanova impregnates the "virgin" in the presence of their hostess. But because he is unhappy with Mlle Corticelli, who behaves more like a dancer than a celestial being, he decides to make the oracle pronounce that "the operation had failed" (8: 47), and that it could only be repeated a year from then. One might conjecture that he also wanted to prolong the wait and thereby dupe the lady a bit longer. In any case, before dismissing Mlle Corticelli, he does not forget to strip her of the jewelry and clothing the marquise had given her.

The following year, in April 1763, they gather again, this time in Marseilles. The ceremony has changed. This time, Mme d'Urfé is to be impregnated and then die while giving birth to a male infant. The progenitor is to be a man named Passano, one of the many adventurers who form Casanova's entourage. Passano, however, becomes too greedy in splitting the spoils and threatens to reveal everything to the lady if he is not satisfied; so the oracle decides to send him off to Lyon. It is therefore Casanova who is to perform the operation. Because he fears "not being up to the task" (9: 55) with a woman he generously estimates to be seventy years old (9: 60) and not fifty-eight as she assures him, he asks for the assistance of Marcoline, his young mistress of the moment, a charming lesbian whom he had stolen away from one of his brothers. To shed the proper light on this episode, we should note that, a few days earlier, Mme d'Urfé had made an offering to the sea consisting of a case that contained seven precious stones of seven carats each in honor of the seven planets (9: 48, 61). Naturally, Casanova took care to send only a substitute case off to the sea and kept the good one for himself.

The new ceremony, refined and meticulous in its complication, is a showcase for the unparalleled erudition of the magician; everything goes exactly as planned, and Mme d'Urfé is so thrilled that she showers Marcoline with gifts. Her only concern is to know who will take care of her in February of the following year, for she is "to die, that is, deliver her child" (9: 70) in January 1764. She therefore makes Casanova this sensible offer:

Marry me, and you will remain the tutor of my child, who will be your son; you will thereby save all of my earthly goods for me and become the master of all that I should inherit from my brother, M. de Pontcarré, who is old and cannot live much longer. If you do not take care of me next February when I am to be reborn as a man, who will? God knows into whose hands I might fall. I will be declared a bastard and lose a fortune of eighty thousand pounds, which you could save for me. (9: 68)

Mme d'Urfé's folly is thus well restrained, for she never loses sight of her financial security. Casanova understands this quite clearly:

I replied that the oracle would be our sole guide, and that I would never stand to see her declared a bastard after she became a man and my son; this soothed her. Her reasoning was quite sound, but because the basis of the argument was an absurdity, she could only provoke my pity. If any reader finds that I should have been a gentleman and disabused her, I pity him, for this was impossible; and even if I could, I would not have disabused her, because it would have made her unhappy. As she was, she had nothing but her illusions in which to revel. (9: 69)

When one learns that Mlle Corticelli had told Mme d'Urfé the whole story, that Passano had written a long letter to give her an authentic account of the facts, and that both had simply been relegated to the camp of mean spirits as a consequence, one might conclude that Casanova was right. On the other hand, if Mme d'Urfé's reasoning is sound, but based on absurd premises, one would have to say the opposite of her companion: his premises are exact, but get lost in sophisms. Once again, he offers us his usual commentary: she would have been duped in any case, so it was better that it be by me. What should be remarked here is that he feels nothing more than pity for her—that is, disdain. He had latched onto her because he knew how to take part in her delirium. She, however, had sparked his own delirium by awakening his infantile omnipotence. Now that he has returned to reality, he sees her as a strange object who no longer plays a supporting role for his imagination. He is impatient to be done with this adventure, all the more so because Passano is after him, and he risks getting in big trouble.

Their last meeting takes place in Paris in June 1763. While in London in August of that same year, Casanova claims to have received a letter from the countess of Rumain announcing the death of the marquise. Now, Casanova must have known that she actually died in November 1775. J. Rives Childs thinks that "what he probably received in August 1763 was a letter notifying him of the withdrawal of her confidence; she was thenceforth dead for him."* Félicien Marceau feels that this is a hasty conclusion; but after reviewing the facts, he despairs of finding an alternative explanation. His objection goes as follows:

In view of the extensive details given by Casanova, I find it difficult to maintain that this death serves here as a simple metaphor. He not only announces that she is deceased, but gives the reason—that she had ingested an excessively strong dose of remedy. He also gives the source of his information: the countess of Rumain. Now, this countess belongs to more or less the same circle as Mme d'Urfé, and an error on her part strikes me as highly unlikely. Moreover, a few pages later, while passing through Tournai, Casanova meets Saint-Germain, who confirms this death and its circumstances. Casanova even says that a wallet containing 400,000 francs was found at Mme d'Urfé's deathbed, whence this sentence that slips out, resembling a regret: "My arms fell listless." Furthermore, he adds that Mme d'Urfé left "a crazy last will and testament, saying that she was leaving her entire fortune to the first son or daughter she bore," and that "she was appointing me to serve as tutor to the newborn." Would this business of the will explain anything?†

But what stops us from suspecting that Casanova might have invented all of these details? He does not, for example, tell us that Mme d'Urfé died from ingesting an excessively strong dose of remedy, but instead "from taking an excessively strong dose of a liquor that she called universal medicine" (9: 250). This medicine is not just any old remedy. In fact, it took the life of Paracelsus, Mme d'Urfé's favorite author: he "had the ill fortune of poisoning himself with an overly strong dose of universal medicine" (5: 107). Moreover, this is the poison ("the same poison that killed Paracelsus"; 5: 120) that Mme d'Urfé wanted to use to die in order to be reborn as a man. If, as the *Memoirs* keep telling us, Mme d'Urfé had lost her senses in this matter, it was completely normal to have

Casanova: A Biography Based on New Documents (London: Allen and Unwin, 1961), p. 175.
†*Une Insolente Liberté: les aventures de Casanova* (Gallimard, 1983), pp. 252–53.

her die in keeping with the logic of her madness. Furthermore, it is quite plausible for Casanova to entrust the countess of Rumain with the task of telling him the news, since she is the only person from Mme d'Urfé's entourage who stayed in contact with him after his departure from Paris in 1759. As for the mention of the will, it results from the combination of two bits of conversation between him and Mme d'Urfé, one held in Paris, before their departure for Pontcarré (8: 40), the other in Marseilles (9: 86)—the two passages are cited above. This is a minor point of erudition (or literary criticism, if you will) that I make to underscore the fact that even those who are convinced that Casanova is an authentic writer have some difficulty in sticking to their convictions at moments such as this, when his art deceives us without warning. He must have had a good laugh, while composing this passage, over the trick he was playing on his readers.

Setting up this scenario, however, was not enough for Casanova. He wanted the so-called death announcement to reach him on the same day as two letters addressed to Pauline, the Portuguese aristocrat with whom he had been happily living for a few months—letters beseeching the young girl to go back home. There is no funerary oration for the marquise because, as Casanova says, he is concentrating his pain and remorse (9: 250) on Pauline's upcoming departure. Thus he marks twice the end of a long stage in his life—the period of his attempts at magic, the period of his happiness. And he recounts a morbid bit of English humor to underscore that the atmosphere has turned somber: he begins the next chapter with the tale of a man who killed himself too early, since his bankruptcy would surely not have hit for another six months (9: 255). This chapter will end by relating Casanova's encounter with Miss Charpillon (9: 276), a courtesan he had met briefly in Paris when she was a little girl to whom he had offered a pair of bracelets (5: 251).

This young woman, who fits so perfectly into the scenery of a London in which Casanova has lost his bearings, sets the tone from the moment she enters the scene. A few months beforehand, Casanova had placed a most singular sign on his door, offering to rent one floor of his house to a girl who spoke English and French. This is how he had recruited Pauline. In the first words Miss Charpillon utters, she reminds Casanova of this odd procedure and adds that, if not for her mother's intervention, she would have responded to the offer herself:

"What need do you have," Casanova replies, "to find inexpensive lodgings?"

"None, but I needed a good laugh and had an urge to punish the audacious author of such a sign."

"How would you have punished me?"

"By making you fall in love with me and then subjecting you to infernal pain through my treatment of you. Ah! How I would have laughed!"

"So you believe that you are able to make anyone you please fall in love with you, and plan in advance to become the tyrant of a man who would have paid a fitting homage to your charms? That is the plot of a monster, and it is unfortunate for men that you do not look like one. I will benefit from your frankness and stay on my guard."

"Your efforts will be in vain. Unless you abstain from seeing me." (9: 279)

A monster who does not look like one. She is indeed a strange apparition, this seventeen-year-old girl with a faultless beauty, a sweet and open physiognomy, who even has a certain noble air about her—but who also decides to make miserable a man who has asked nothing of her. She brusquely intrudes on the scene because she wants to avenge the fair sex. She seems to say: by putting up such a sign, this man has demonstrated his disdain for my sex, and I will get my revenge. To a certain extent, there is no duplicity in her, for she announces her goal and her strategy, and even goes so far as to predict Casanova's only recourse: flight. Part dove, part vulture, she knows her power over men, but wants to use it only to destroy them. Sure that she will never feel love or tenderness, that she is incapable of pity, she recognizes that she is filled with the most relentless kind of hate for this man, whose reputation as a lady-killer is well established.

How did Casanova manage once again to come up with precisely the kind of woman he needed, at just the right moment? Although he has never really met her, ever since his childhood encounter with Bettine, he has always sought and always fled this particular persona: the true witch, not a witch of the order of sweet, pathetic, gullible Mme d'Urfé, but rather the real witch—the evil spirit of fairy tales, who can assume the appearance of a pretty girl and then, all of a sudden, turn into a horrible old toothless hag with the menacing laugh of a madwoman. It is when faced with such a vulture that our libertine admits his defeat. He can no longer fall back on the cabala or magic as a means of protecting himself with superior powers; he has lost the flamboyant youthfulness that once allowed him to turn his back on suffering or quickly escape its grip, and he has renounced his old faith in destiny and acknowledged that he is responsible for his own actions; in a word, he no longer knows how to deceive people and has lost any inclination to fool himself. All that he has sought lately is to push his audacity a bit further. And here he finds that Miss Charpillon far outdoes him. In her insolence, she is a champion who knows no rival. She is expert in deception because she is irresistible and has no need to don a mask; rather, she announces her plans quite plainly and never wastes a minute bothering with remorse, exonerating herself, or making excuses. At the age of seventeen, she is in the bloom of youth, full of promise and still growing. She is a lovely little spider who will devour this gnat after ensnaring him with her charms.

The initial reason that Casanova is fatally seduced by Miss Charpillon is that she reflects a certain mirror image of himself. They are undoubtedly different, for he has been in love, whereas she is full of hate; he is generous, whereas she takes and gives nothing; he tries to nurture happiness, whereas she wants to make people suffer. Yet has he not also haughtily bought countless women and sought to subjugate many others by demanding that they love him? Miss Charpillon appears at this moment in order to pay him back for his disdain. More important, however, he is fascinated because she has no fear of men and attacks them straight on with no subterfuge except her beauty and wit. Casanova, in contrast, has often trembled before women, for in order to love them he has always been obliged to bow and scrape and take labyrinthine detours. He cannot take his eyes off of this intrepid woman, who shows him what it means to have the opposite sex at one's feet without feeling any emotion—which would indeed be dangerous. As a consequence, she can exploit her victim without running the risk of getting too involved or injured. In this, at least, Miss Charpillon recalls Casanova's successful adventure with Mme d'Urfé, whom he has (conveniently) just sent off to her grave. In a few days, however, Casanova's situation is reversed. He could proudly contrast his thirty-eight years to the hopeless fifty-eight years of the marquise. But now that circumstances have changed, what claims can he make for his relatively advanced age in the face of Miss Charpillon's adolescent maturity? Because he insists on taking up her challenge, he is doomed. After his first meeting with her, he solemnly announces: "It was on this fatal day at the beginning of September 1763 that I began to die, and stopped living" (9: 279–80). And a bit later, when his adventure has brought him closer to the precipice, he writes, "This is what love did to me in London *Nel mezzo del cammin di nostra vita* at the age of thirty-eight.* This was the end of the first act of my life" (9: 315).

How can one recount this heartbreakingly sad story, a tale that takes up almost 80 pages of the *Memoirs*? It can be summed up in a few words: Casanova is convinced that the spell will be broken as soon as he succeeds in sleeping with her, which he must do as quickly as possible; Miss Charpillon is obviously of the same opinion, which is why she makes endless promises but always arranges to postpone going through with it. Casanova has been forewarned about this by his friend Milord Pembroke, who can speak from experience: "She is a rascal who will do everything in her power to ensnare you" (9: 282).

Miss Charpillon returns to visit Casanova at his home, spends several hours there, and then invites her victim to lunch the next day. Surprise: the girl lives with her mother and aunts, the same women who, in 1759, had swindled their host of the evening by paying him with fake vouchers. There are also three "professional rogues" present. As Casanova writes, "I saw myself introduced into this infamous society, and although I noticed their dubious character straightaway, I neither left nor vowed never to come back" (9: 283). He convinces himself that this bad lot is not involved in his intrigue.

Three days later, Miss Charpillon asks him for 100 guineas so that her aunt can prepare a "life-giving balm." He tries to seize this occasion to make a move on her, but she gets away. She warns him

---

*Dante's *Divine Comedy*, canto 1: "In the middle of the journey of our life."

that he will never get anything "through money or violence," but that he can "have the highest hopes for her friendship" as soon as she sees him "behave as sweetly as a lamb when alone with her" (9: 285). He is about to give up his efforts to seduce her, when her aunt takes charge and promises him that her niece will be accommodating, and that he can come to see her right away. He hurries there; the young beauty, who is taking a bath, refuses to receive her visitor and orders that he leave. He nonetheless gives the 100 guineas to the aunt.

Goudar, one of the rogues, is sent to speak to Casanova and suggests that he make a bargain. When she hears of this, however, Miss Charpillon is outraged: "Bargaining is out of the question. What I want to know is whether you think you have the right to insult me, and whether you believe that I am not sensitive to such an insult." A true lady! And she goes on, "Know that I love you, and that it makes me very unhappy to see you treat me this way" (9: 295). She then suggests that he court her for two weeks. He accepts, takes the whole family out every day, and spends a small fortune. When night falls, he finds her wrapped in an impenetrable shift. No matter how much he shouts, pleads, rages, and rips, he gets nowhere. They fight, and he scratches her. The mother and aunts protest. He apologizes profusely, and is full of remorse and disgust with himself.

The game goes on in the same manner. The alternating of assurances of love and refusals continues on both sides. Each time that he meets all of her conditions and thinks that he has reached his goal, she drives him off or shuts herself away. Each time that he gets furious, refuses to see her, and disdains her too much to think of touching her, she becomes smiling and coy. A classic scenario, is it not? It goes on until the day when Casanova finds her in bed with her hairdresser and smashes everything in her mother's house. Miss Charpillon has a crisis, and her entourage claims that she is ill, that she is on the verge of dying, and, finally, that she has passed away. Casanova writes, "At that moment, I felt an icy hand pressing my heart" (9: 327).

He puts his personal affairs in order and fills his pockets with lead weights, "with the firm intention of going to the Tower of London and drowning myself in the Thames." He cannot stand to stay alive, for he would find himself "in infernal torment each time that Miss Charpillon's image came to mind" (9: 328). When he is halfway across Westminster Bridge, however, he meets the knight Egard, who, upon seeing him in such a state, refuses to leave him and invites him to spend the evening with him. They end their stroll in a cabaret. Casanova nearly falls ill: Miss Charpillon, whom he thought to be dead, is there before his eyes, dancing with great gusto and wearing a dress and hat that he had given her. In a single stroke, he is finally cured of his love. He tries to avenge himself by having her mother arrested; but this move backfires, and he must negotiate a compromise. He gets real revenge thanks to a parrot that he teaches to say the following sentence and then takes out on the streets: "Miss Charpillon is a bigger slut than her mother" (9: 348).

Throughout this story, Casanova is nothing but a puppet whose strings are pulled by Miss Charpillon and her entourage. He reacts to every move just as she had predicted, like a truly well-controlled automaton. So what has happened? If this woman's supposed death prompted preparations for his own suicide, he must have ceded all his power to her. As he tells us many times, although he could regain his senses when they were apart, he was bewitched once again at the sight of her. What does she do to hypnotize him? She simply keeps herself from feeling any desire for him. She charms him with her presence without ever feeling the slightest echo of the sexual agitation she is arousing. In this sense, she has attained a rare perfection. Although she is not frigid—rather, she is sexuality personified—her neutrality is total. The sight of such a contrast, movement in repose, captures the gaze and holds it tenaciously.

Casanova is also fascinated by something else. Miss Charpillon wants respect; she wants to be loved even while succeeding in returning neither love nor respect. How often he has complained that his reason was overcome by his senses! Now he has before him living proof that the contrary is possible; so he undertakes obstinately to destroy this proof. The two engage in a combat of Titans. She wants to rout this figure of male self-importance who reduces all women to uniformity and erases their identities. He, however, would like to do away with this difference confronting him, so inaccessible, so impervious, so perfectly distinct. She is stronger than he because she has no desire for him and can thus resist his relentless effort to confuse her identity with others. This woman is an archetype. She proclaims, in effect: "If you call me a trollop, I will double the stakes and be nothing but that, and you, sir, will be beaten with your own weapons; I'll make you, the great libertine, look like a fake who will impress no one but dreamy-eyed school-girls. No harem for you, just me; you can pant after me all you want." She might be called a harlot, but because she is insensitive to love, she is transformed into an avenging vestal virgin.

It is the impossibility of overcoming this unbearable difference that drives Casanova to the brink of madness. After recovering from his foiled suicide attempt, he explains that one commits suicide to avoid losing one's mind (9: 330). He was unwittingly led astray because he had not grasped from the beginning that, through his notorious reputation, he had come to personify the myth of libertinage and was therefore the enemy this woman had always dreamed of meeting and slaying. Needing neither his money nor his caresses, she could show him that, like many women, she was not interchangeable. When he sees her, radiant, in the cabaret that morbid evening, she does not make the slightest gesture to exonerate herself or ask forgiveness; for she was probably savoring the results of her work, a bitter tonic for a man dying of thirst. After such a good day's work, she had the right to go dancing.

Let us not do Casanova the injustice of thinking that he did not understand what had happened to him. He knows that he has lost the game, but he can learn only those aspects of the lesson that suit his system. That is, he will apply Miss Charpillon's coldhearted method in his usual manner, to destroy the specificity of women.

He learns that a lady from Hanover is in London with her five daughters, in a state of great destitution. These girls are all pretty and will have to go out begging on the streets in order to survive, but he would not think of coming to their rescue. Casanova sets out in their pursuit, and one of his first questions is, fatally, "Are these more Charpillons?" In the course of this episode, which he conducts with cynicism and boundless insolence, the image of the woman who trampled him underfoot comes back like a refrain. No one could accuse him this time of letting his pity be aroused. He explains the mechanism of his libertinage to one of the girls who asks him to help her: "I told her that Miss Charpillon had cost me

2,000 guineas, and that she never even granted me a kiss, but that the same thing would not happen again." And when he sees the mother, he remarks, "I found her rather similar in appearance to Miss Charpillon's mother" (10: 3). A bit later, he tries to bargain with this same lady: "Miss Charpillon will be the last woman to ensnare me" (10: 5). He is truly obsessed. After a short while, these girls prove to be accommodating; he claims that he had all of them in succession, and that the last and youngest daughter was the best. He is probably boasting a bit here, for according to historians, this family did indeed have five children, but only three daughters.

This adventure, which served as a postscript to his foibles with Miss Charpillon, is a harbinger of something else. After having dared to say to the mother, "Madam, I am a libertine by profession, and if I had daughters, I am sure that they would have no need of a preacher" (10: 3), he sets down this remark to conclude the episode:

If I had been rich, these Hanoverians would have kept me in their clutches until my dying day. I seemed to love them not as a lover, but as a father, and the thought that I was sleeping with them posed no obstacle to this sentiment, since I have never been able to understand how a father could feel a truly tender love for his charming daughter without having slept with her at least once. My inability to conceive of the idea always convinced me—and convinces me even more forcefully today—that my mind and body are made of a single substance. (10: 17–18)

As we shall see, although these remarks are made in passing, they are hardly casual.

Social Order Through Incest

WITH THE PAIR of childhood recollections related at the very beginning of the *Memoirs*, Casanova indicated that his entire life would be marked by two things: bleeding,* which identified him with women (that is, the witch and the bedeviled madwoman), and the need to dupe the father. As we have seen, it is precisely these two questions that haunt him throughout his life, although they may take varying forms and, at times, intersect: first, the question of woman as a being different from himself, whom he must reduce to sameness; and second, the question of the authority of the law, which hampers his infantile omnipotence. After testing a series of more or less effective solutions, Casanova will try another, more radical solution, which should (theoretically) settle the two questions in one fell swoop—namely, the practice of incest. Clearly, the very foundations of society are affected by this practice; moreover, the resulting confusion of generations brings with it the effacing of all differences.

Leonardo Sciascia is, to my knowledge, the only critic who has focused on the seminal role played by incest in the literary composition of the *Memoirs*. As he writes, "After a certain point in my

* Blood is mentioned frequently throughout the *Memoirs*, be it bleeding from the nose or from the penis after prolonged sexual intercourse, at the moment when "the woman's genitals are no longer different from one's own." See, among others, the episodes at 1: 125; 2: 228, 245; 4: 69; 7: 14, 236; and 8: 180.

rereadings, I began to wonder more and more persistently whether one could not consider Casanova's work as a little universe, a 'system' revolving around the idée fixe, which becomes the utopia, of incest."* This may seem a slightly hasty extrapolation, even though one can demonstrate, as I have in the preceding chapters, that Casanova's most pressing preoccupations are likely to converge on this theme. Sciascia's remarks are nonetheless worth noting, for they give the writer the full stature he deserves and suggest that, as we shall see (and, oh, how clearly), he did not venture onto this terrain unprepared.

In discussing the passage from the *Memoirs* that explicitly treats incest, Félicien Marceau professes to a certain irritation with the episode's insipid quality, "the absence of any circumstantial incident or, more precisely, of that unforeseen detail that can abruptly crystallize a story and give it a flavor of truth."† With a critic who is usually so adept at recognizing the essence of a text, we can only take him at his word. It may be that Casanova adhered more to an idea or principle than to experience in treating the subject of transgression through incest—an idea or principle that was, in fact, a commonplace in eighteenth-century literature; and, omnivorous reader that he was, it is unlikely that Casanova could have been unfamiliar with this theme or failed to notice how well it could serve his purposes.

For, in the end, it matters little whether we know that incest actually occurred or not, whether it was commonplace during this period or not. Although such questions are clearly interesting, they are secondary to our concerns and best left to moralists. What is important is to determine what Casanova says about incest, how he introduces and presents the subject—in a word, what he does with incest as a writer to complete his self-portrait. As we shall see, this question is introduced almost imperceptibly in the *Memoirs*, and then elaborated through a most skillful progression.

Here is his first discreet brushstroke: he is in Aix-les-Bains at the end of 1760 and meets one of the countless doubles who periodically cross his path, the son of Marquis Desarmoises, a gambler by

---

*"L'Utopie de Casanova," *La Nouvelle Revue Française*, no. 336 (Jan. 1, 1981): 1–11.

†*Une Insolente Liberté: les aventures de Casanova* (Gallimard, 1983), p. 309.

profession. Desarmoises recounts his very particular tale of woe: "My house is in Lyon, but I never go there because of my oldest daughter, with whom I am unfortunately in love. And because of my wife, I cannot make her listen to reason." Casanova replies, "That is quite a story. If it weren't for your wife, do you think that she would take pity on her enamored father?" And his companion confirms: "It is quite possible, for she has a very good character" (6: 253)—which inspires this remark from the author of the *Memoirs:* "As I strolled to the fountain with this man, who did not know me and hence spoke in perfect good faith without the least fear of repulsing me or appearing a first-class scoundrel, I reflected that he must have assumed I was a kindred spirit who would be greatly honored by his confession" (6: 254). It is of course the other man who assumes Casanova is "a kindred spirit," so he alone is responsible for this supposition. The confession of Desarmoises does not, however, fall upon deaf ears. A year later, the Venetian passes through the region once again and is entrusted by Desarmoises with the task of bringing his daughter back to Lyon, for she had been taken all the way to Chambéry by her young lover; Casanova seizes the occasion to play, for a few days, the role that his comrade so longs to play for her (7: 287–96).

But these are merely appetizers; things are going to get a bit more serious. Between the two events mentioned above, which occur early in 1761, Casanova goes to Naples, where he had not been since his horrible journey of 1743. He is received at the residence of the duke of Matalona. The next day, the duke introduces him to his titular mistress, a girl of eighteen named Leonilda. The duke, however, keeps her as his mistress only "for the sake of appearances" (7: 213), since he claims to be impotent with all women save his spouse. The path is clear. Casanova wastes no time in falling in love with Leonilda; and with a haste that is not typical of him under such circumstances, he decides to marry her, even though nothing decisive has happened between them. She accepts. Everything is arranged in a matter of days. They send for the notary and await only Leonilda's mother. By a dramatic turn of events, this mother turns out to be none other than Donna Lucrezia, whom Casanova had met with her husband, the lawyer, and her sister Angelica, during his first journey from Naples to Rome. With dates in hand,

Donna Lucrezia proves to Casanova that Leonilda is his daughter: "My husband never touched me in Rome, and my daughter was not born prematurely" (7: 229). She concludes by saying that this marriage horrifies her, and cannot refrain from asking whether they "had already consummated it before the ceremony." "No, my beloved friend," replies Casanova; and Leonilda goes even further: "I never loved him except as a daughter" (7: 230). Anguish, trembling, tears, sadness—all the ingredients of a great tragic scene are present. Casanova takes advantage of them to interrupt his tale with reflections on the incest taboo—a passage that is worth quoting in its entirety, so well does it illustrate his libertine mode of functioning:

Along the way, the duke was the only one to speak, and he made a number of reflections on what is known as prejudice in moral philosophy. There is no philosopher who would dare say that the union of a father with his daughter is something inherently horrible, but the prejudice against this is so strong that one must have a completely depraved mind to trample it underfoot. This prejudice is the fruit of the respect for the law that is instilled in an honest mind by a good education; and, so defined, it is no longer a prejudice, it is a duty.

This duty can also be considered natural, in that nature inspires us to grant our loved ones the same benefits that we desire for ourselves. It seems that what best suits reciprocity in love is equality in everything—in age, in condition, in character—and at first sight one does not find this equality between father and daughter. The respect that she owes him who gave her life poses an obstacle to the kind of tenderness she must feel for a lover. Should the father attack his daughter by using the force of his paternal authority, he would be exercising a tyranny that nature must abhor. In orderly, natural love, reason also judges such a union monstrous. One would find nothing but confusion and insubordination in its results; hence such a union is abominable on all counts; but it is no longer abominable when the two individuals love each other and have no idea that reasons foreign to their mutual tenderness should prevent them from loving each other, so rather than making me cry, incest—the eternal subject of Greek tragedies—makes me laugh, and if I cry at *Phèdre,* it is purely because of Racine's art. (7: 231)

Casanova starts by having the duke express what he himself thinks, as would any other Enlightenment philosopher: to declare the union of a father and his daughter horrible is the fruit of a prejudice. If one is properly educated, with a mind free of depravity, this prejudice becomes a duty. As he begins a new paragraph, Casanova seems to speak in his own voice: duty in love supposes an equality that cannot exist between a father and daughter. Their union is tyrannical, monstrous, abominable. You must certainly agree. And presto! a pirouette, a semicolon, and morality and duty disappear; this union is not abominable if the two love each other and are not aware of the interdiction that applies to them. A second pirouette, a simple comma this time: from the Greeks to modern times, incest has always made me laugh.

This page is a masterly hoax on the reader. If one reads it quickly, one gets the impression that Casanova is defending the reigning opinion of his day before mocking it. His method, however, is more cunning and also more complicated. First, by letting the duke speak, he subscribes quite explicitly to a tradition typical of his century—the practice, popular among some philosophers, of ridiculing the incest prohibition. This reinforces the thesis that Casanova's interest in this subject derives from what one might call the cliché or trope that had to be espoused by anyone who aspired to write high literature—a thesis that by no means contradicts the theory that Casanova actually committed incest. What is clever in this passage is that, first of all, Casanova lets the duke speak; then, without indicating who is speaking, he takes up the cause of defending the prohibition; and, finally, without changing the sentence and especially not the tone, he overturns this entire defense with laughter, specifically the laughter of a spectator. We are back in the theater, and incest becomes a subject for tragicomedy. Casanova may criticize the incest prohibition, but he takes care to situate his criticism in the realm of literary fiction. As he tells us, he dismisses the horrible aspect of incest not to encourage its practice, but, rather, to show that it holds great potential as a topic of literary fiction.

This story might seem invented, for we have never seen Casanova take the risk of marriage quite so far; even the notary had been summoned. He had gone as far as asking C.C.'s father for her hand in marriage, but he knew full well that the proposal would meet with a refusal. Furthermore, before taking that step, he had taken the precaution of "getting married" in secret. In this case, apparently, he does nothing of the kind; although the duke is ready to

cede Leonilda to him, and Leonilda eagerly grants her consent, they
await the official ceremony before consummating the marriage.
This is truly a departure from our hero's usual behavior, particularly
since Leonilda does not exactly keep him at arm's length. She will
show that she is not the least bit shy in a short while.

While reminiscing with Lucrezia about their days in Rome, Casanova recalls their erstwhile passions; they fall into each other's arms. In the morning, Leonilda arrives, undresses, and lends
the two lovers her support. Lucrezia is careful to make Casanova
extinguish his fire in herself. The flame spreads nonetheless, without true incest ever being committed: "She allowed me to cover
all that I could see with my kisses; but as soon as I was on the
edge of the precipice, she would dodge me and hand me over
to her mother, who welcomed me with open arms" (7: 236). In
a word, Leonilda plays a role similar to that played earlier by
Angelica, Lucrezia's sister, in relation to Lucrezia—and even more
similar to the role played by Marcoline in the regeneration of
Mme d'Urfé.

A few years go by. In 1763, Casanova is in Milan when he meets
up with Count and Countess Rinaldi, a sordid couple who had
robbed him at the gambling table (2: 201–2). He tells us here that
at the time of their earlier acquaintance, the countess excelled at
"the art of leading him on during their intimate encounters, while
granting him nothing." Now there appears in Milan a young woman
of sixteen named Irène, who calls him Papa. Casanova asks her
mother, the countess, where Irène had been born:

"In Mantua, three months after I left Venice."
"When did you leave Venice?"
"Six months after making your acquaintance."
"That is curious. If I had had a tender liaison with you, you could tell
me that I am her father; and I would believe it, and judge the passion she
stirs in me to be our blood speaking."
"I am surprised that you forget certain things."
"Oh, oh! I tell you that I never forget matters of this sort, but I see
everything. You want me to reject the feelings she inspires in me, and I
shall do so; but she will be the worse for it."
Irène, who had been struck mute upon hearing this short conversation,
regained her composure after a moment and told me that she resembled me.
"Stay," she said to me, "and dine with us."

"No, for I might fall in love with you, and a divine law prohibits me from doing that, according to your mother's claim."

"I was joking," replied the mother. "You can love Irène with a clear conscience."

"I believe it." (8: 171)

In the days that follow, Irène will become his mistress. Historians, and J. Rives Childs in particular, doubt that Irène was actually his daughter. Doubt, however, is essential at this moment in the story. This is the subtle interpretation suggested by Sciascia:

In truth, Casanova does not in the least "see everything"—or else he does not want to allow us, his readers, to see everything. The situation is simply left there: the countess was joking and he got the joke. Had he been less of a "Casanovist" and more of a critic, Rives Childs would have noticed this and resolved the doubt—once more in Casanova's favor. A game that might appear nonsensical is in reality quite subtle when set down in a book: Giacomo Casanova playfully offers us a symbolic anticipation—an opening of sorts—of the actual consummation of the incestuous relationship he will recount in the last chapter of the eleventh volume without any veil or the slightest sense of guilt. At this moment, Casanova the character does not know what will happen with his daughter Leonilda in Salerno in August 1770, but Casanova the writer knows full well.*

As if to underscore the ambiguity of his relationship to Irène, the tale of this adventure is interrupted for a moment by his encounter with Bellino-Thérèse, who introduces him to their son, Cesarino, whom she passes off as her brother (8: 175). Because Cesarino bears an uncanny resemblance to Casanova, it is implied that Casanova was once on intimate terms with Cesarino's mother—that is, the woman who would be seen in the eyes of the public as the mother of Thérèse. Although none of this constitutes incest, Casanova seems to delight in truly muddling generations.

In Marseilles in that same year (1763), just as he has explained to Marcoline that "I am going to England to try to take my daughter out of her mother's hands" (9: 88), Irène suddenly reappears. Sciascia remarks: "As well as serving as a fictive prefiguration of a real transgression, Irène's arrival triggers a veritable family orgy in the *Memoirs. . . .* The kinship ties are nominal, fictive; but the en-

---

*"L'Utopie," p. 4.

joyment that Casanova procures from these names, these fictions, is without question real and true."* Casanova had come from Milan with a girl whom he passes off as his niece and always refers to as "my niece." Marcoline, who had been mistress to Gaetano Casanova before passing into Giacomo's arms, is also there. Marcoline, the ex-future-sister-in-law, who had slept with the "niece" (9: 28), now sleeps with Irène, the daughter, and Casanova sleeps with both of them (9: 92).

If one notices that this intricate set of relationships is elaborated around "the grand operation" that Casanova is to perform on Mme d'Urfé, one might suspect, and with reason, that they have a further significance. Casanova is no longer interested in magic at this point; he is instead intent on setting the stage for the actual act of incest. And given that Mme d'Urfé is twenty years older than he, she strikes me as an excellent candidate for a mother figure. Casanova's relationship to Leonilda, which had changed into a relationship to her mother, Lucrezia, can be paralleled to his difficult sexual union with Mme d'Urfé, accomplished only with Marcoline's assistance. What appears here is nonetheless *not* incest with the mother—about which Casanova cares little—but, rather, incest with the daughter. In fact he has the marquise pronounce the same ritualistic words that Leonilda will use later: "Tomorrow, my dear Galtinarde [that is Casanova's name during the magic operation], you will be my husband and my father [because she is supposed to give birth to herself]. Ask the scholars to explain the enigma" (9: 62). Mme d'Urfé has no further importance for him, except in the context of his grand scheme, his utopia. We can now see why he gradually modified the ritual of the great operation—first rejecting the idea of transporting the marquise's soul into that of Thérèse Imer's son, then abandoning the project of having a son born from his coupling with Mlle Corticelli, and finally taking the place of Passano so that he himself could be the agent to impregnate Mme d'Urfé. These are modifications that critics do not even attempt to explain, yet that seem quite significant on the whole. Casanova has accustomed us to the technique of illuminating a higher design through tiny brushstrokes, which, by themselves, go unnoticed.

*Ibid., p. 5.

Casanova set out, then, for London in hopes of rescuing Sophie, the daughter he had had by Thérèse Imer (9: 88). According to Rives Childs, the real goal of his trip was to establish a lottery like the Paris lottery.* Is it not curious that Casanova does not make the slightest mention of this in the *Memoirs*? Might that not be a clue to the goal he is now pursuing in his writing? With Sophie we can justly suspect that his "fiction" appears well before 1761. As early as late 1758, when he meets Thérèse in Holland, she introduces him to his daughter and explains that they had been together as lovers on Ascension Day in 1753, and that Sophie was born at the end of that year (5: 135). Casanova's behavior is not ambiguous: "Once I had taken her on my lap I could not keep myself from smothering her with kisses. In her silence, she was delighted to see that she interested me more than her brother did. She was wearing nothing but a very light petticoat. I kissed every part of her pretty body, charmed by the thought that I was the man who had given this creature her existence" (5: 144). And a bit later: "I left after having devoured my daughter with kisses. I would indeed have liked her mother to give her to me, but my pleas would have been useless, for I saw that she considered the girl a resource during her eventual old age" (5: 148). Was it not in fact Casanova himself who was thinking along these lines, who would have paid a pretty penny to take her from her mother (5: 166)?

Let us return to London in 1763. Casanova's first visit is to Thérèse Imer. Sophie is now a ten-year-old girl, forced by her mother to observe rigid manners that displease Casanova. One day, he puts her to bed with Pauline and tells her that he will bring her breakfast in bed the next day to see whether she is just as pretty then as she is when dressed. There follows a scene that is even less ambiguous:

Laughing gaily, Sophie hid under the blanket when she saw me coming; but as soon as I jumped on the bed near her and started to tickle her, she stuck out her little face, which I covered with kisses, and I invoked my paternal rights to get a full view of how she was made everywhere and to praise all that she had, which was still quite green. She was very small, but ravishing. Pauline watched me giving Sophie all of these caresses without suspecting that there was the slightest bit of malice involved, but she was

* *Casanova: A Biography Based on New Documents* (London: Allen and Unwin, 1961), p. 185.

mistaken. If Pauline had not been there, Sophie would have had to extinguish one way or another the fire that her little charms had sparked in her papa. (9: 215)

Sophie complains repeatedly about her mother's severity and even falls ill from it. Casanova sees no other solution but to put her in a boarding house, where she is in fact happy, and where he frequently goes to visit her—every day even, when he is seeking to console himself from the rebuffs of Miss Charpillon (9: 286). At the end of his stay in London, we may recall that he had said to the mother of the Hanoverian girls: "Madam, I am a libertine by profession, and if I had daughters, I am sure that they would have no need of a preacher" (10: 3). It is easy to infer that Casanova actually has Sophie in mind here. He goes so far as to invite her one day to join his little harem: "Sophie went from one Hanoverian to the next, each of whom devoured her with kisses" (10: 13). It is in this context that we should reread the text cited at the end of the last chapter, in its entirety this time:

I was also philosophizing, but sadly; I saw myself near the end, and thought of Lisbon. If I had been rich, these Hanoverians would have kept me in their clutches until my dying day. I seemed to love them not as a lover, but as a father, and the thought that I was sleeping with them posed no obstacle to this sentiment, since I have never been able to understand how a father could feel a truly tender love for his charming daughter without having slept with her at least once. My inability to conceive of the idea always convinced me—and convinces me even more forcefully today— that my mind and body are made of a single substance. Gabrielle's eyes told me that she loved me, and I was sure that she was not deceiving me. Who could possibly think that she would not have felt this sentiment if she had had what one would call virtue? For me as well, the idea is incomprehensible. (10: 17–18)

In this passage, Casanova suggests one of the reasons underlying his fascination with incest as the juncture point of several crucial problems. He poses, first of all, a question whose solution (when one puts aside all of the prejudices instilled by "education and custom"; 11: 177) is far from obvious. The "at least once" forces us to wonder not, of course, whether he is referring to a desire that has no object—for that is nonsense—but, rather, whether desire can exist without being already realized in part, without becoming effective to a certain extent. Casanova has never been able to conceive of the possibility of love without sexual desire or of sexual desire without realization, because he cannot conceive of a dichotomy between body and soul: the two go together. But if this is so, one must consider the consequences and acknowledge that virtue, or what is socially recognized as such, is opposed to feeling and desire. Here, then, is the question he asks himself in the form of an aporia: how can one reconcile the necessity of incest, which is necessary to preserve desire and love, with the imperatives of virtue, by which society seeks to prohibit incest in order to uphold itself? This is the question that Casanova will now address, in his usual serious manner.

It is August 1770, and Giacomo is forty-five years old. He is about to leave Naples for Rome; but when he learns that Donna Lucrezia and her daughter Leonilda—now marquise de la C.—are in Salerno (11: 306), he decides to pay them a brief visit. Upon arriving, he takes a room in a nearby inn and sends a note to Lucrezia. She rushes over within a half hour, as if the passage of this shooting star were a godsend; indeed, this woman does not seem to be lacking in determination. She explains right off to her former lover (in 1744 and 1761) that her son-in-law, the marquis, would be very happy to see him, and that her daughter's only woe is to be childless: "It is unfortunate for her, because all of her husband's wealth will go to his closest relatives at his death" (11: 309). Leonilda, the daughter, welcomes the visitor with open arms, unhampered by the presence of her husband, who is well aware of the past situation. As for Casanova, he immediately announces his sentiments quite clearly: "She was my daughter, and far from preventing me from having all the feelings of a lover for her, nature prohibited me from having nothing but the inconsequential sentiments of a father" (11: 309). The marquis does likewise; he embraces his guest and even gives him a kiss on the mouth. They recognize each other as brother Freemasons. Casanova discovers, however, a more particular affinity, as if the marquis were serving here to define Casanova's own behavior in the events to come: "Like her, he was a freethinker, but in the greatest secrecy, for no one in Salerno had an open mind; hence he lived with his wife and mother-in-law like a good Christian and adopted all the prejudices of his compatriots"

(11: 310). Casanova knows full well that, as other civilizations have done throughout history, one must distinguish between incest practiced secretly, which can be quite beneficial to a family, and incest revealed to the outside world, which gives rise to shame and the undoing of social ties. And in his own peculiar way of never touching anything on the social surface—even as he preserves his full liberty to think and act—Casanova is perfectly adapted to this situation.

He takes a tour of the house, which is always cool in this torrid month of August, and visits the paradisal gardens with their flowers, their waterfalls, their grottos adorned with seashells, their ornamental ponds, their covered walkways. Casanova, who hardly ever describes the landscape, waxes lyrical here. He has another conversation with Lucrezia who, with all of her maternal grace, reaffirms what this oaf might not yet have grasped—that the marquis's greatest misfortune is to have no successor, for he does not like his nephews:

> "They are all ugly and sullen," she [Lucrezia] told me, "and have been raised like peasants by provincials and ignorant priests."
> "But is your daughter really happy?"
> "Very happy, even though she cannot find in the husband she adores the lover she probably needs at her age."
> "This man does not strike me as capable of jealousy."
> "Indeed, he is not jealous, and I am sure that if she could have found a man to her liking among the nobility of this town, the marquis would have welcomed him like a cherished friend, and deep down he would not have been angry to see her become pregnant."
> "Is he positively sure that if she gives him a child, he could not be its father?"
> "Not altogether, for when he is feeling well he comes to sleep with her, and according to what my daughter tells me, he could flatter himself and take credit for what he might not, in fact, have done." (11: 312–13)

One could not accuse this group of mincing words. In any case, these two connivers have set the stage for the upcoming scene. The task of the progenitor has been made absolutely clear: he is sure to make everyone happy and to suffer no repercussions, since appearances will be saved. These are two conditions that suit Casanova perfectly. And now, let the play begin.

Next appears the young marquise Leonilda, who asks him to extend his visit and come stay with them in the country for a few days. He accepts the invitation. The trio—Casanova, Lucrezia, Leonilda—go into a grotto: "We indulged in the pleasures of calling each other by the tender names of daughter and father, which authorized us to take certain liberties that, although imperfect, were nonetheless slightly criminal" (11: 315). Leonilda reminds Casanova that, whereas she had been free in 1761 as titular mistress of the duke of Matalona, she is now duly married. As for her mother, Lucrezia, she gives them a lesson in morality before leaving the pair alone together so that what she is condemning in advance can in fact take place. And since by now everyone has played out the farce for himself and for the others, the big event can finally arrive, in Casanova's peculiar high style:

> But her words, followed by her departure, had an effect quite contrary to the precept she was preaching. In our determination not to consummate the so-called crime, we got so close to this point that an almost involuntary movement forced us to consummate it so completely that we could not have gone any further if we had acted out of a premeditated design. We stayed as we were, immobile, looking at each other without changing position, both of us serious and speechless, lost in thought, astonished, as we told each other later, to feel neither guilt nor remorse. We fixed our disheveled attire, and my daughter, seated next to me, called me her husband just as I called her my wife. We confirmed what we had just done with sweet kisses; and even if an angel had come along at that moment to tell us that we had committed a monstrous outrage against nature, we would have laughed. Absorbed as we were in this very decent tenderness, Donna Lucrezia was edified to find us so tranquil. (11: 315–16)

The utopia of incest is no longer merely the general fashion of the century in this episode; it is the particular style of a writer. This passage contains certain characteristics reminiscent of Casanova's first sexual experience, with Nanette and Marton. In both episodes, the determination not to act is the necessary condition for the act to be committed involuntarily and forcibly. And as Casanova emphasizes, the fortuitous act is nevertheless as complete as if it had been premeditated. The effect of this cunning combination—and these are truly Casanova's words—is to produce neither guilt nor remorse. As for the reminder of proper morality, it can once again only provoke laughter.

Although deception is generalized here, no one is anyone's dupe. Casanova and Leonilda agree, without saying so, to keep their encounter a secret because they realize that Lucrezia left them alone "merely to be sure that she would not witness what we were about to do" (11: 316). She would like to believe that they "went no further than childish games." The comedy reaches its finale with the entrance of the old marquis, who swears that he feels "ten years younger" thanks to his visitor, and promises his wife, Leonilda, that he will pay her a visit that night. With the tact that we know so well, Casanova tops off the evening with one last word: "I left at that point with Donna Lucrezia, after expressing my hope that they would have a handsome son nine months from that date" (11: 317). And the marquis performs his duties admirably that night (11: 318).

Casanova must, however, cover his tracks. Although he renews his tender attentions to Leonilda, he must pretend to be interested only in Anastasia, the "chambermaid": "We agreed that I would go into her apartment only to woo Anastasia" (11: 319). Lucrezia is pleased, for the marquis must not suspect that Casanova is coming to see his wife. Casanova plays his assigned role to the hilt, primarily because, when Anastasia is sleeping, he can pass through her room to Leonilda's. After a few days, however, our progenitor—who must have been a bit too attentive with Anastasia—falls asleep instead of joining the marquise. When the marquise learns this, she simply laughs, which does not stop her from tracking Casanova down "two or three times in a secluded spot in the garden, for a hasty encounter" (11: 324).

This laugh from Leonilda, who is not in the least bit jealous, and the insistence of her mother, who needs a grandson to assure the security of her old age, set this story of incest into the most bluntly Casanovian register: whether or not Casanova is her father, Leonilda needs a stud above all; and when she learns that this rare bird is in town, Lucrezia does not miss her chance. Casanova's crudity is displayed here in all its glory, since he is well rewarded for his practical joke. In fact, the marquis asks him to accept the dowry of 5,000 ducats that Casanova had returned to his daughter after their

aborted marriage. The little marquise is too delicate to handle this
transaction herself: "She thought that you would find it in bad taste
for her to use this sum to release herself from the debt of gratitude
she owes you" (4: 325). The phrase "gratitude she owes you"
sounds odd coming from the lips of the marquis, but not from the
marquise—for a little heir will be worth much more to her than
5,000 ducats. After all, this is not a very high price, particularly
since it is the marquis who is paying.

But that is not all. The marquis not only pays the instrumental
man, but also offers Donna Lucrezia a gift of the same sum for the
services she has rendered to the cause: "Leonilda and her mother
cried tears of joy when, in their presence, the marquis gave me five
thousand ducats in bank bills, and at the same time gave another
five thousand to Donna Lucrezia as an expression of thanks for having introduced him to me" (11: 326).

Casanova goes on his way quite sadly. But what pleasure he must
have had in writing us such a tale, well after the fact—all the more
so because he has played yet another trick on his readers. When he
tells us that "Leonilda gave birth to a boy in May" (12: 72), he also
mentions that he met the lad twenty years later and was struck by
"how much the boy resembled the late marquis, husband of his
mother." And he adds: "This reflection brought tears to my eyes,
when I thought of how satisfied the good marquis must have been
with this resemblance, not to mention the boy's mother" (12: 73).
How much one can make of resemblances! They serve here to mis-
lead readers just a tad more, to blur their view and recollections. So
this boy may be the marquis's son after all, and nothing may have
happened between Leonilda and Casanova. Casanova does not want
his readers to find their way out of the maze.

Be that as it may, having taken so long to set up this story, he
wants us to leave it with one indelible impression: provided that it
is kept and practiced secretly—and that one remembers to erase the
traits of the progenitor in favor of those of the father—one can
hardly call incest monstrous; it is a lovely, fine thing, because its
consequences ensure hereditary succession and fortune, in a word,
the stability of the social body. It is the veritable motor of society,
which is all the more effective because it obliges us to espouse the
optimal hypocrisy—the foundation of all human relations.

Even if this utopia seems somewhat artificial, especially in the final scene, Casanova does not merely espouse it as would any well-versed man of his century. He is too intent on muddling generational distinctions—and by implication, all distinctions of gender and identity—to overlook this means of accomplishing it. However, to avoid being judged guilty of this transgression, he has to prove to himself that incest was a great blessing for everyone.

The *Memoirs* end with Casanova's reunion with his daughter Irène and with Marcoline, who serves as a passing reminder of Mme d'Urfé. The last sentence suggests one last incest, committed with Irène's daughter, that is, the possible granddaughter of Casanova: "At the beginning of Lent, she [Irène] left with the rest of the troupe, and I saw her three years later in Padua, where I made a much more intimate acquaintance with her daughter."

Library of Congress Cataloging-in-Publication Data

Roustang, François.
  [Bal masqué de Giacomo Casanova. English]
  The quadrille of gender: Casanova's "Memoirs" / François Roustang;
translated by Anne C. Vila.
    p.   cm.
  ISBN 0-8047-1456-8
  1. Casanova, Giacomo, 1725–1798. Mémoires. 2. Casanova, Giacomo,
1725–1798. 3. Europe—Biography. I. Title.
D285.8.C4R6313   1988   87-27807
940.2′53′0924—dc19   CIP